CU00751245

A Practical Guide to Play Thi in the Outdoors

A Practical Guide to Play Therapy in the Outdoors responds to the significant and growing interest in the play therapy community of working in nature. Alison Chown provides practical ideas about why we might decide to take play therapy practice into outdoor settings and how we might do this safely and ethically.

This book discusses how nature provides a second intermediate playground and can be seen as a co-therapist in play therapy. It explores the relevance of different environments to the play therapy process by considering the elements of earth, air, fire, water and wood. It looks at the way we can connect with nature to find a sense of place and details some activities to do with children in play therapy to get started.

The book provides an important guide for the practitioner and talks them through the crucial guidelines that are necessary for outdoor play therapy and gives a philosophical perspective to working in nature. It will be engaging and essential reading for play therapists in training and practice.

Alison Chown is a play therapist and experienced specialist teacher for children and young people with complex social, emotional and mental health difficulties. She is an independent practitioner and director of Phoenix Play, and its sister company Learning Tree Training Limited. She has lectured at Foundation Degree level in Behaviour for Learning, Developing Inclusive Practice and Child Development and was an associate tutor for Worcester and Plymouth Universities. She has been a visiting tutor at the Romanian Institute of Play and Dramatherapy and is the author of *Play Therapy in the Outdoors*. Alison is also a certified Beach School practitioner.

A Practical Guide to Play Therapy in the Outdoors

Working in Nature

Alison Chown

Routledge
Taylor & Francis Group

LONDON AND NEW YORK

First published 2018
by Routledge
2 Park Square, Milton Park, Abingdon, Oxon OX14 4RN

and by Routledge
711 Third Avenue, New York, NY 10017

Routledge is an imprint of the Taylor & Francis Group, an informa business

Before practising play therapy outdoors, readers should ensure they fulfill all legal, ethical, safeguarding and health and safety requirements and duties. They should also have the appropriate insurance cover and first aid training. Neither the author nor the publisher take any responsibility for the consequences of actions taken as a result of the information and guidance contained in this book.

Trademark notice: Product or corporate names may be trademarks or registered trademarks, and are used only for identification and explanation without intent to infringe.

British Library Cataloguing in Publication Data
A catalogue record for this book is available from the British Library

Library of Congress Cataloguing in Publication Data
A catalogue record for this title has been requested

ISBN: 978-1-138-65661-1 (hbk)
ISBN: 978-1-138-65679-6 (pbk)
ISBN: 978-1-315-54570-7 (ebk)

Typeset in Times New Roman
by Out of House Publishing

For John, whose love, support and encouragement holds me always.

Remembering Martin Jordan

As I came towards the final stages of writing this book in January 2017, I was shocked and deeply saddened to hear of the untimely death of Martin Jordan. I only really knew him through his writings but met him briefly when he invited me to give a key note speech at Brighton University where he taught. His work has inspired my thinking, particularly his book *Nature and Therapy*, and he walks within these pages. He will be greatly missed by all whose lives he touched.

Contents

Figures

Foreword

I am honoured to write a foreword for this remarkable book. Alison Chown has managed to weave a wonderful tapestry that holds the reader on tenterhooks all the way through.

She skilfully presents historical and contemporary theory which underpins her practice and integrates it with her in-depth practice of play therapy in the outdoors. Her practice with individuals and groups sits firm on a bedrock of accepted theory and then takes us on a dance through a playful landscape. Much of the time the book reads as if she is giving us a personal tutorial, giving practice examples at just the moment we might have asked a question.

Alison guides us through crucial issues of personal motivation to practice beyond the walls, our aims and objectives and the important issues of Health and Safety. I particularly like her description of using the elements in outdoor play therapy: fire, earth, air, water, wood and ether. Her experience of application shines through her examples and we know they had successful resolutions.

Although much of her work is of a unique and pioneering nature, Alison is almost self-effacing in the modesty of her writing. However, I believe it is essential that this philosophy and practice are taken very seriously and disseminated as widely as possible. We have such responsibility for children who are damaged or vulnerable, and now we have an approach that can really make a difference.

Nature and play come together with joy in order to provide a healing context for children to hurt less and play more. I cannot recommend this book too highly. Indeed it is a treasure chest that will continue to provide jewels to the therapist and their children.

Professor Sue Jennings PhD
Glastonbury, Somerset
2017

Disclaimer

This book is intended primarily for qualified Play and Creative Arts therapists, those in training and those supervising therapists who are interested in working outdoors or who have already moved their practice into outdoor environments. However, it is anticipated that it will also be of interest to other professionals who work with children and young people in a variety of settings and capacities such as Forest School practitioners, teachers, early years providers, social workers and psychotherapists.

In the case of those professionals other than qualified and practising therapists, it must be made clear that this book is not intended to train you as a therapist but by engaging in playful outdoor activities with those with whom you work, you may well be offering experiences which have a therapeutic quality and the activities contained within these pages will be helpful and even valuable to those who are involved in them. It is also an inherent aspect of safeguarding that you are aware of your own limitations and know when you must refer on to your line manager or another professional organization.

Play therapists undergo extensive and comprehensive training at postgraduate level in a number of key areas including child development, children and young people's mental health, play therapy skills and competencies and working with children, their families and other professionals. They complete a research dissertation requiring the understanding of various research methods and carry out at least two clinical practices with full supervision. In most cases, they will also be required to have personal therapy for the duration of their course in order to address any underlying personal issues which may interfere with the processes of their clients and to give them a direct experience of the therapeutic process they will take their clients through. Crucially, both personal therapy and supervision are a key issue for those wishing to move their practice into the outdoors as will be explored in more detail later in this book.

Author's notes

In academic circles there is much discussion about the difference between the terms 'place' and 'space'. However, within this book, the terms are used somewhat interchangeably. This is also true of the terms 'client', 'child' and 'young person'.

Acknowledgements

As always, my thanks go to all those children and young people who have shown me what true courage is in the giving up of their stories. They are my inspiration and without them, this book would not have come into being.

My thanks go to Sarah Holden, Loz Foskett, Penny McFarlane, Janette Parker and Marion Woodward who have so generously given their time to talk, read and comment; I am grateful for their honesty and enthusiasm for the topic and their support for the writing process. My thanks also go to Joanne Forshaw at Routledge for believing this book was worth pursuing.

I am grateful also to my daughter Rhiannon for her photograph for Wood, and to my son Jack for his illustrations of the 'halfway houses'. Together we have spent many happy days 'spuddling' in nature and their company is always a treasured memory.

Finally, my gratitude goes to Sue Jennings who has been my supervisor, colleague and friend for many years. She is a font of wisdom and knowledge and has been tireless in her support of my 'pioneering'! I cannot imagine that I would have stepped beyond the playroom door with such vigour had it not been for her gentle nudgings.

Introduction

My decision to work with nature in outdoor places came after a number of years of working indoors as a non-directive play therapist and was set against a background of experience in outdoor education and work with young people with complex social, mental health and emotional needs. It followed a lot of soul searching. I had had numerous conversations about using the outdoors and yet maintaining ethical standards such as confidentiality and the integrity of the work with a valued colleague and friend of mine. Out of the blue, she sent me an article from the 2010 *European Journal of Psychotherapy and Counselling* by Martin Jordan and Hayley Marshall entitled 'Taking counselling and psychotherapy outside: Destruction or enrichment of the therapeutic frame?' The article focused on holding the therapeutic frame beyond the therapy room, in natural places, and gave particular consideration to the issue of confidentiality through contracting with the client. Although Jordan and Marshall worked with adult clients, there it was in black and white – other therapists had been working in outdoor places and had explored the ethical issues at some length.

Further discussion with my supervisor raised the question not of 'why go outdoors?' but 'why not?' I kept coming back to 'frame' issues; 'what if there are other people around?' ... 'how do I maintain confidentiality?' ... 'what if I can't get the child back inside?' ... 'what if there's an accident?' ... and so on! My supervisor was somewhat perplexed by these questions since I had been working outdoors with children in an educational context. 'Yes but surely with therapy it's different?' And yes it is different but there are some distinct similarities in that whatever capacity you are working in with children, when you go outdoors there are some basic considerations to be made, which will be discussed in chapter 5 of this book.

What my supervisor and I focused on was the needs of the client and, as always, the importance of holding these as central to any decision making about practice issues and processes. I don't know what conversation Martin Jordan and Hayley Marshall might have had en route to moving their work outside but I suspect, like me, they had the weight of years of traditional thinking within the profession upon them which says that the only safe space in which to practise most forms of therapy is a closed room which contains only the client and the therapist (Chown 2014).

I like Nick Totton's way of viewing therapy in outdoor places when he considers that it is as different to working indoors as camping is to living at home (2014). I think this view frees us up to think differently about our work, not to compare one environment with the other in order to see what is missing but to consider what Totton goes on to describe as the significant and beneficial differences and what these mean to the process, the client and to ourselves. If you like being in outdoor places, you may be a camper and embrace nature and all she has to offer or you may prefer the relative luxury of a hotel bed. It matters not. What does matter is how you *feel* about being outdoors – what meanings do the places and spaces that you visit hold for you?

For me as a former specialist teacher for children with social, mental health and emotional needs, a further point for consideration was whether there is a difference between therapeutic play and play therapy, often used interchangeably, and if, in moving outside, we also move between one and the other or from one to the other. I think it is important to clarify this here so that we can all be confident that if we are play therapists doing play therapy in the indoor play room, we are still play therapists doing play therapy when we are working in nature. Whilst this book may be of interest to those who work in a broader but more generally therapeutic capacity with children or who use play within any setting, play therapists have a particular set of skills and competencies which differentiates their work from other play practitioners.

There is an argument to say that all play is broadly therapeutic – that it can be relaxing, beneficial, satisfying and restorative to the person engaged in it as a self-initiated and self-directed activity. Once you add another person in the form of a mediator, someone who is there to facilitate the play process, then perhaps there is greater potential for the process of play to be therapeutic since the mediating adult such as a playworker may have an understanding of the process involved. The play might then be enhanced through discussion of the *child's* ideas and the *offering* of additional resources to enable them to extend their play. However, the therapeutic quality of the play is significantly reduced if the mediating adult attempts to direct it in any way and undermines the child's autonomy. Where the play is a goal oriented intervention to achieve an improvement in some aspect of a child's behaviour the facilitating adult may be said to be a therapeutic play practitioner, although again, this will depend on the level of direction the adult gives. Where the play remains self-chosen and self-directed, then we might say it borders on play therapy but where the adult mediates the play to meet an agreed outcome or objective, then for me this remains therapeutic play.

There are many attuned, open and accepting adults who are part of our clients' lives, particularly within the school setting, but most are charged with meeting some kind of predetermined objective, for this is the way of education these days – measurable outcomes which show progress by which both the child and the school can be evaluated and judged. So what is the extra dimension that play therapists bring that turn a therapeutic activity into therapy? Many of us will have some kind of objective for our work, agreed with parents and/or those who commission our work, but it is the non-directive approach we use, allowing the child to lead, coupled with comprehensive training and particular personal characteristics which come from life experiences and which have been explored in both personal therapy and supervision, which differentiates those offering play therapy. As a play therapist I need to remain open and non-judgemental, to respect the child for who she is and what she brings – to see us as having equal potential in the process we are embarking on. Landreth (2002:100, original emphasis) tells us that:

> Effective play therapists have a high *tolerance for ambiguity*, which enables them to enter into the child's world of experiencing as a follower, allowing the child to initiate activity, topic, direction, and content with encouragement from the therapist, who continually centres responsibility [for this] on the child.

I think this is the bit that sets play therapists and play therapy apart from therapeutic play, this ability to trust the child completely which goes hand in hand with our feelings of personal security and allows us to accept and recognize our personal limitations and frailties without feeling we are inadequate in any way. As part of most therapeutic training we must undergo personal therapy which supports this sense of personal security and raises our awareness of our own values, anxieties, emotional needs and personal biases (Landreth 2002) so that we are better able to recognize those of our clients and to take our own issues to either personal therapy or supervision so they do not interfere with our clients' process.

I am clear that what I do when working outside in nature is play therapy – it does not change just because the location changes. This is so whether I am working with an individual client or a small group. We may be accompanied by other adults, some supervisory and others working therapeutically in the broad sense, but I am the play therapist and how I interact with the children is different.

So why is this so important? Those children whose lives have not gone according to plan have differing needs deserving of attention from a range of practitioners who each have something different to offer. Play therapy, for the reasons set out above, is a particular and very different way of working with children. We need to maintain our professional difference not so that we can say we are better than anyone else, but so that when children need a space that is theirs alone in which they can safely explore their fears and anxieties within an accepting relationship which does not demand them to behave in a certain way or address particular issues, play therapy is the obvious answer.

Professional status should not be seen as something which allows us to command excessive fees or to hold ourselves above others. It should be seen as a commitment to be the best we can be for our client group because that is what they deserve. It should be a mark of both our individual and collective integrity.

We live in a rapidly changing world and the pressures on our young people are mounting, not least as a result of a growth in the use of technology. Two years ago, Dawn Rees, Principal Policy Adviser for Future in Mind, highlighted the difficulties they face in her guest blog for the Children's Commissioner:

> They still have the same developmental, relationship and resilience challenges, but the world around them has changed. The pressures of learning, poverty, inequality, bullying, social media, unemployment, gangs and sexual exploitation exert impossible pressures on them – especially the most vulnerable – and often they are invisible to us.
>
> (2015)

Within society, but particularly at governmental level, there appears to be little recognition of the fact that the children and young people of today are the adults of tomorrow and any investments we make in them, in time, energy, commitment and finance, can only pay dividends in the future. While recent pledges from central government to increase spending on mental health are welcome by all, the news has to be set against cuts to the budget in the name of austerity over nearly a decade which will mean any increases merely taking us back to where we started from. All lives are precious, but none more so than children's and they deserve better. They deserve good quality education that is not driven by unrealistic target setting. They deserve to be part of families where employment hours are guaranteed and wages realistic in relation to the actual cost of living. They deserve to grow up in suitable housing, not over-priced rented accommodation with little security of tenure. They deserve clean air and open spaces and to be able to play out safely. They deserve to be valued as children, not exploited as consumers. And when their emotional and mental well-being is compromised, they deserve to have access to high quality support that is appropriate to their needs and not just an off-the-peg, best-fit intervention at the cheapest available price. To take account of an ever changing society, we as practitioners also need to play our part; to be open to change and not afraid of it and to see our practice as dynamic, offering new direction when it is needed. Taking play therapy beyond the playroom and into nature is one such change of direction, arising out of client need and forging a new pathway, but one that is badly needed.

Although the number of play therapists working in the outdoors is steadily increasing, there is still little being published about it. The writing of this book has come about largely from feedback from those who have attended my workshops or come across my first book and asked for ideas on how to get started. The book is structured in a particular way so that the practical guidance is set in the context of continually developing practice and under-pinned by widely accepted theory and concepts about play and its role in children's development. It is not a 'programme' of a fixed number of sessions each containing activities to do with the children. It is in many ways more a philosophy of play therapy in nature and as such contains aspects of a num-ber of different perspectives.

Chapter 1 briefly considers the development of play therapy from the early child psychotherapy of Anna Freud and Melanie Klein through the work of Virginia Axline, whose guiding principles still inform our work today, to cur-rent practice including animal-assisted therapy and my own work in the out-doors. It underlines how practice is dynamic, shaped primarily by our clients' needs and our own experience of finding ways to meet them and how this gives rise to the generation of new theories and concepts. A point of interest here that arose from researching the history of play therapy relates to gender balance. In a profession where the key founding figures were women, and where the major-ity of practitioners are female, a disproportionate number of those credited with being significant to the development of both the profession and practice in the USA appear to be male. In the UK, however, the story is very different with the key players being female, representative of the gender breakdown of practitioners as evidenced at any play therapy training or conference.

Chapters 2 and 3 consider why there is a clear rationale for including access to outdoor environments in the practice of play therapy. Two key issues are addressed. Firstly, *chapter 2* discusses the concept and purpose of play, focus-ing on the role of play in healthy childhood development, highlighting the importance of a healthy 'body self'. The difficulty in reaching a single def-inition for play is discussed and links between theories and concepts about attachment, play, social learning and child development are made in relation to play therapy practice. Consideration is also given to the issue of the 'where and how' of play and how this changes as we grow and develop.

Secondly, *chapter 3* details how we have arrived at a position of needing to actively promote outdoor play and physical activity amongst our children, discussion which demands a more sociological perspective. It considers the importance of risk in developing social, emotional and mental well-being underlining how safety measures have undermined creative play. It discusses how the 'where and how' of play has changed over recent decades from play in adventure playgrounds to play in commercialized spaces and the rise of screen-based play. It explores how policy changes as a result of changes to the government have resulted in play being used as an assessment tool both in itself and as part of evaluation systems for successful service delivery.

In highlighting these two key themes, it should be noted that they are not separate issues, but are interconnected, since in a developing society, social, health, educational and planning policy must surely take into account the necessity of play in children's lives, and in adults' since they in turn influence the 'how and where' of play. Since we live both in and as part of nature, this needs to be reflected in all aspects of policy making in order to facilitate a more authentic relationship with her so that we come to see her not merely as a resource for exploitation and commercialization but recognize our dependency upon her for survival and understand that her survival depends on shifting prevalent attitudes in global society.

Chapter 4 discusses how nature or 'the nature mother' can provide an enhanced sensory experience which offers rich symbolism and metaphor for our inner worlds and our relationships with our self and others, and allows a more democratic context for play therapy. It discusses the idea of a sense of 'place' which arises out of our individual relationships with or attachment to particular landscapes and places. It is a synthesis of several ways of viewing outdoor spaces and places and nature within them including literature from nature writers and cultural philosophy.

Chapter 5 contains guidance on preparing to work outdoors and what practical aspects you will need to consider including safeguarding, insurance and first aid. The structure for the chapter comes from topics arising from my workshops and in discussion with colleagues, and covers questions, such as:

- Where or how do I start?
- How long do I work with a child before moving outside?
- Should I expect to work outdoors with every client?
- How do I decide if *I* am ready?

Chapter 6 invites you to meet the five elements of water, wood, earth, air and fire in a range of landscapes. Each section considers the potential of the environment in relation to play therapy processes and practice, some basic health and safety pointers and includes a narrative which considers some of the symbolism and metaphors offered by nature. These narratives are for you to use as you will; to read to yourself or to your clients, to adapt or change them as necessary but above all to whet your appetite for working in nature.

There are ideas for helping you and your clients to get to know each landscape and also for activities which you can use with either individual clients or small groups. These will help you all to become comfortable with being outdoors, to enjoy being together and to have fun. You can use them across the different environments and again change or adapt them, particularly if your clients have sensory, mobility or learning needs. Consideration is also given to small spaces and other places and the idea of 'halfway houses', small structures that act as playrooms but are outside in nature for when your client needs a defined and contained space to work in.

In *the appendices*, there are various bits and pieces including guidance on risk assessment, additional health and safety advice, a resource list, a sample 'can you spot?' list and a checklist of things to do before you go outside.

Finally… this book is not instructional. It has not been written with the intention of telling you that you must move your play therapy practice outside or, if you do, that you must do it in a certain way. It offers guidance and suggestions to encourage you and to support your decision making. I believe you will find it useful and I hope it will inspire you. Those of us who have already taken a step through the playroom door know it was the right thing to do for the child/ren we were working with. Hold the client as central to what you do and they will show you the path you need to take. If we are encouraging our clients to take a risk with us, we need to know we can take a risk with ourselves so take your first steps with courage and just a little trepidation, for this will keep your mind sharp but your heart open to all that nature has to offer.

References

Chown, A. (2014) *Play Therapy in the Outdoors: Taking Play Therapy out of the Playroom and into Natural Environments*. London: Jessica Kingsley Publishers

Jordan, M. and Marshall, H. (2010) Taking counselling and psychotherapy outside: Destruction or enrichment of the therapeutic frame? *European Journal of Psychotherapy & Counselling* 12 (4), 345–359

Landreth, G. (2002) *Play Therapy: The Art of the Relationship* (2nd edition). Hove: Brunner–Routledge

Rees, D. (2015) *Guest Blog from Dawn Rees, Principal Policy Adviser: Future in Mind*. Available from: www.childrenscommissioner.gov.uk/news/guest-blog-dawn-rees-principal-policy-adviser-future-mind [Accessed 12th January 2017]

Totton, N. (2014) The practice of Wild Therapy. *Therapy Today* 25 (5) (June). Available from: www.bacp.co.uk/docs/doc/15199_tt ed june 14.doc [Accessed 9th January 2017]

Chapter 1

A brief history of play therapy

Early beginnings

Even a brief history of play therapy needs to start with Sigmund Freud who famously documented the case of little Hans in the first published account in 1909 of the use of therapeutic play. Although he worked primarily with adults, Wilson et al. (1992) suggest that his observations on the meaning of children's play were noteworthy for the contribution they made to later thinking, and in particular to that of his daughter Anna and her contemporary Melanie Klein. However, we need also to recognize the contribution of the Austrian psychoanalyst Hermine Hug-Hellmuth in the early 1900s, considered to be the first to work with children and provide them with play materials with which to express their internal world, thus conceptualizing play therapy – through play, children are able to communicate unconscious experiences, thoughts and feelings without the need for words or structured language.

Both Anna Freud and Klein, working from the 1920s onward, were considered pioneers in child psychotherapy, highlighting the relationship between children's spontaneous play and free association used in adult psychoanalysis and recognizing that the cause of childhood psychiatric disorders was, in the main, unconscious conflicts which might be resolved when they were brought into the conscious by the therapist's interpretations of the play and of dreams. There were differences to the approaches they developed, since Klein believed all play to be symbolic whereas Freud saw play as enabling the child to talk about their conscious fears, thoughts, anxieties and feelings while unconscious matter would be played out and that in doing so, the child was not necessarily playing symbolically but could be re-enacting real situations. Because Freud considered play enabled the child to verbalize in the manner of free association in adult psychoanalysis, she did not consider children under the age of seven suitable for therapy. However, she did see the need to create a strong relationship with the child in order to gain access to their inner world although this was in a more dependent way than the 'neutral' relationship we seek to establish today in non-directive play therapy (McMahon 1992).

Klein's approach acknowledged the importance of the relationship between the mother figure and the infant and the idea that our inner world is constructed from our early mental processes. Because she saw nearly all play as symbolic, Klein relied heavily on interpretation and believed that the role of the therapist was to explore the child's unconscious through reflection on the transference in the relationship the child made with the therapist. She also saw that the relationships children make in infancy impact on development although she saw development as occurring throughout the whole of life and as such contributed significantly to the field of developmental psychology. Despite the differences in their approaches almost resulting in a split during the 1940s within the British Psychoanalytical Society, Wilson et al. (1992) suggest that their contribution to the field of understanding and working with children has greatly influenced those who followed them, with the range of toys and resources used by Klein and the non-directive nature of her approach to the child's play continuing to inform play therapy today.

Whilst Klein's playroom was well resourced with a range of miniature figures, simple, non-mechanical toys, drawing and painting materials, paper, scissors, glue and water (Landreth 2002, McMahon 1992), sand play, a staple ingredient of play therapy today, was developed by Margaret Lowenfeld, a contemporary of Freud and Klein. Lowenfeld, a child psychiatrist, had recognized the importance of play to children's development and understood that language was frequently an inappropriate medium for their expression of thoughts, feelings and experiences. She developed a non-verbal means of expression for children to use in therapy known as the 'World Technique' whereby children used a sand tray and miniature objects depicting all aspects of their lives to create small worlds to explore their own inner workings (lowenfeld.org no date). In addition to a large rectangular tray, water and pieces of plasticene were also available for children to construct landscapes for the vast range of miniatures she stored in drawers. Interestingly, rather than coming from a psychotherapy perspective, she noted that her greatest influence was H. G. Wells, and in particular a small book he had written describing the floor games his sons constructed using their toy soldiers and wooden blocks (Science Museum no date).

In the 1950s, Dora Kalff, a Swiss Jungian analyst worked with Lowenfeld and secured her agreement to develop her own style of working with sand which she called sandplay which also incorporated aspects of Eastern philosophy and Neuman's system model. Sandplay is grounded in Jungian psychology and *'helps honor and illuminate the client's internal symbolic world, providing a place for its expression within a safe container'* (Friedman and Rogers Mitchell 2005). The approach emphasizes the importance of the therapeutic relationship in facilitating the client's awareness in the present and analysis of the sandplay takes place after the session. This is in contrast to sandtray therapy, developed by Linda Homeyer and Daniel Sweeney, where the therapist is the facilitator and moves from a position of observation to reflection during the session. They describe their approach as:

> an expressive and projective mode of psychotherapy involving the unfolding and processing of intra and inter-personal issues through the use of specific sandtray materials … led by the client or therapist and facilitated by a trained therapist.
>
> (2017:6)

Sandtray therapy also differs from sandplay in that it is cross-theoretical and thus considered to be more adaptable. However, both approaches serve to illustrate how differing theoretical perspectives lead to the development of new or alternative ways of thinking about both the process and practice of therapy and how client needs can inform and generate new theory.

Whilst some may suggest that we 'stand on the shoulders of giants', we need to accept that this position enables us to see ahead and to develop what has gone before in the light of our own experiences so that each and every one of us has the capacity to become a 'giant' and add to the development of both theory and practice.

A client centred non-directive approach

For child centred play therapists, it is the work of Carl Rogers and Virginia Axline which underpins the non-directive method of play therapy we currently employ. Rogers was an American psychologist in the 1940s, who was part of the growing humanistic psychology movement. From this approach, he considered a new style of working with clients, where the perception of the therapist as the 'expert' was replaced with the idea that the person themselves has an innate 'actualizing tendency' which drives them towards the achievement of their full potential.

> This new tradition was born as a protest against the diagnostic, prescriptive perspectives of that time … As such, the person centred approach posited a new and original theoretical perspective of personality structure, psychological health, acquisition of psychological difficulty and the change process within therapy.
>
> (British Association of Play Therapists (BAPT) 2013)

This person centred approach recognizes that humans are biologically predetermined to seek contact with others as a means to survival and so our ability to make and sustain fruitful relationships, to know others and to be known by them is key to our physical and psychological well-being. However, it was Abraham Maslow, a contemporary of Rogers, who was the pioneer of the idea of human growth towards what he termed self-actualization, the idea *'that our purpose in life is to go on with a process of development which starts out in early life but often gets blocked later'* (Rowan 2005).

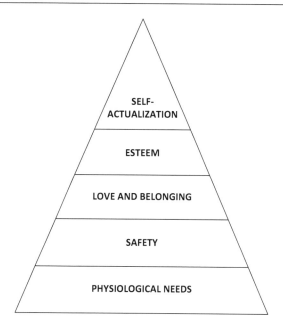

Fig 1:1 Maslow's hierarchy of needs (1943)

Rogers considered that for growth to occur we need to be open to experience, to trust and be trusted, to be curious about the world and have the capacity to be creative and compassionate. To create this healthy state, we require a safe and secure environment, one where we receive unconditional positive regard from another who is empathic and able to be their true self with us, to be congruent. The idea that there are certain conditions which are required for human growth and development echoes Maslow's formulation of the idea that there are levels of need we must satisfy or meet before we can grow and ultimately self-actualize (see fig 1:1). The first four levels of the pyramid can be described as deficiency needs and are comprised of our basic physical and psychological needs which must be adequately met before we can meet our self-fulfilment need and achieve our potential (1943).

One of the key aspects of a person centred approach is that it does not rely on specific techniques but on the non-judgemental relationship established between the therapist and the client that is the therapeutic alliance. This in turn relies on the personal qualities of the therapist and their ability to stay with the client in a congruent manner which allows for that relationship to grow and develop in an atmosphere of trust and empathy. This in turn suggests a much more equal and democratic relationship than in the earlier psychoanalytic approaches and one predicated on the notion that rather than the client being in the hands of the therapist, they know what they have to do to 'heal' themselves and are in an environment where the conditions for this healing and subsequent growth allow for a greater degree of autonomy.

Although Rogers' approach was initially used within counselling and psychotherapy, it was extended into education where it became known as student centred learning and was further developed in group situations such as large commercial organizations. In this way, it might be regarded as a forerunner of today's coaching movement which also emphasizes the individual's learning, development and growth potential as a way of stimulating critical thinking and new ways of being, supported by the relationship with the coach within a non-judgemental environment. (United States Department of Agriculture no date). Although the names Rogers and Maslow are those that spring to mind when we think about personal growth and self-actualization, the UK Association for Humanistic Psychology Practitioners (UKAHPP) reminds us that this is a rather reductionist view and that there were other key people in the human psychology movement at the time including Fritz Perls, founder of Gestalt therapy, Alvin Mahrer, who developed existential psychotherapy, Rollo May, who focused more on the tragic dimensions of life, and Jacob Moreno, who conceived and developed the idea of psychodrama as a means to facilitating insight and personal growth.

Another contemporary of Rogers and Maslow was Clark Moustakas who worked as a play therapist, and published *Children in Play Therapy* in which he also emphasizes the importance of the relationship:

> Play therapy is a relatively new field of human endeavour ... Techniques, tools and methods play a large role in therapy. But the particular values of the therapist pervade the relationship and, to a large degree, determine its therapeutic effectiveness.
>
> (1973:1)

He goes on to note that play therapy may be thought of as a set of attitudes which can be transmitted from one person to another and may be learned, although not taught. These attitudes – faith, acceptance and respect – are not imparted through any clear-cut formula, but reflect the therapist's own life experiences and so are blended imperceptibly into the relationship. Some forty years later, I found myself echoing Moustakas' thoughts in my own book, *Play Therapy in the Outdoors*:

> On reflection, I think it is not about identifying skills we have and that we might teach someone, for implicit in having to teach them, the notion of authenticity and genuineness already seems compromised. It is more a case of who we are; the sum of our life experiences.
>
> (Chown 2014:121)

Virginia Axline's non-directive play therapy approach was heavily influenced by Rogers' person centred approach and the core conditions of authenticity, non-possessive warmth and accurate empathy (Wilson et al. 1992) and her eight underpinning principles, reflective of Moustakas' 'attitudes', still guide the work of non-directive play therapists today.

Axline's eight basic principles of non-directive play therapy (1969)

The therapist must develop a warm, friendly relationship with the child, in which good rapport is established as soon as possible.

The therapist accepts the child exactly as he is.

The therapist establishes a feeling of permissiveness in the relationship so that the child feels free to express his feelings completely.

The therapist is alert to recognize the *feelings* the child is expressing and reflects those feelings back to him in such a manner that he gains insight into his behaviour.

The therapist maintains a deep respect for the child's ability to solve his own problems if given an opportunity to do so. The responsibility to make choices and institute change is the child's.

The therapist does not attempt to direct the child's actions or conversations in any manner. The child leads the way; the therapist follows.

The therapist does not attempt to hurry the therapy along. It is a gradual process and is recognized as such by the therapist.

The therapist establishes only those limitations that are necessary to anchor the therapy to the world of reality and to make the child aware of his responsibility in the relationship.

Whilst *Play Therapy* is crucial reading for any therapist, Axline's seminal book *Dibs in Search of Self* is an inspiring and moving account of her work with a particular small boy whose behaviour baffled the professionals around him to such an extent that they were left unsure of whether he was 'mentally retarded', autistic or gifted.

> When he started school, he did not talk and he never ventured off his chair. He sat there mute and unmoving all morning. After many weeks he began to leave his chair and crawl around the room, seeming to look at some of the things about him. When anyone approached him, he would huddle up in a ball on the floor and not move. He never looked directly into anyone's eyes. He never answered when anyone spoke to him.
>
> (Axline 1964:10)

Dibs not only provides us with critical evidence of the efficacy of the non-directive process, but also shows us why it is so important to keep faith with both the child and the process.

The 'art' of the relationship was further explored by Garry Landreth in his book of the same name (2002) which develops Axline's original principles and considers the detail of a way of being with children which enables the development of the therapeutic relationship and facilitates the play therapy process. Landreth founded the Center for Play Therapy at the University of North Texas in 1988 in response to the university's commitment to make play therapy a focus for national training, underlining both the growing importance of children's psychological well-being and the expansion of the field of play therapy. Landreth has also developed a programme of Child Parent Relationship Therapy which emphasizes the importance of the parent/child relationship in children's well-being and is based on the work of Bernard and Louise Gurney.

> In a supportive group environment, parents learn skills to respond more effectively to their children's emotional and behavioral needs. In turn, children learn that they can count on their parents to reliably and consistently meet their needs for love, acceptance, safety and security.
>
> (Center for Play Therapy no date)

The original approach developed in the 1960s by the Gurneys was known as filial therapy and involved parents directly as the agents of therapeutic change. Through training, parents learned structuring, empathic skills, limit setting and imaginative, non-directive play skills which enabled them to take the play therapy sessions with their child whilst the therapist observed, facilitating parent and therapist discussion of the session afterwards. Parents as partners in play therapy is one of the ways in which the process has been adapted to provide differing models which also include aspects of narrative therapy, cognitive behavioural therapy, systemic family therapy and other creative arts therapies.

Although coming from a psychology background, Charles Schaefer is considered by many to be the father of play therapy in America. He has written extensively about aspects of play and children's development as well as both the theory and practice of play therapy and co-founded the Association for Play Therapy (APT), established in 1982. APT's broad aims are to promote the value of play, play therapy and credentialled or qualified play therapists. The professionalization of play therapy through accredited postgraduate training and recognition by professional bodies is crucial to ensuring the widest possible access for children and families. The mission statement of APT emphasizes the necessity for public understanding, effective and evidenced practice and the development of strong professional organizations as key to promoting the value of both play therapy and play therapists and for advancing the psychosocial development and mental well-being of all people (APT 2016). Schaefer was also the founder and co-director of the New Jersey-based Play Therapy Training Institute, one of many international institutions currently offering both training and continuing professional development in the field of play therapy. To mark his contribution to the field of play therapy The Association for Play Therapy awarded him both the Distinguished Service Award in 1996 and a Lifetime Achievement Award in 2006 (Farleigh Dickinson University 2006).

Developments in the UK

A word about Winnicott

Before looking at the roots of play therapy in the UK, it is important to look at the work of Donald Winnicott and its influence on our understanding of the infant/ mother figure relationship and the importance of play to children's healthy development. Winnicott, a paediatrician and psychoanalyst during the 1930s and 40s, conceptualized the idea of the 'holding environment' provided by the ordinary loving care of the ordinary mother. He considered the holding, bathing, feeding and changing activities she engages in as fostering the idea for the infant of the body as the place where one can live securely. He also put forward the idea of the 'potential space' between the mother figure and infant as the place where play and playfulness develop, positioning it between inner and outer worlds, the inner world of both mind and body in partnership and the outer world of reality (Winnicott 1971). The quality of the play and playfulness will depend on the experiences of the infant in relation to the mother figure. Winnicott emphasized play as crucial to the development of the 'true' self, our capacity for feeling alive inside. In playing, we feel real, spontaneous and creative, in touch with ourselves and our bodies. Without the experience of a positive, loving and caring relationship with our mother figure, we may develop a 'false' self, one that is defensive and protective and which leaves us unable to make and sustain fulfilling relationships but instead leaves us dead within, incongruent in our responses.

Although Winnicott's therapeutic work was largely psychoanalytical, he also practiced psychotherapy but stressed in *Playing and Reality* that he would not wish to draw a clear distinction between the two when considering the role of play in the therapeutic process. He draws a parallel with the play of the mother figure and infant in describing play in therapy:

> Psychotherapy takes place in the overlap of two areas of playing, that of the patient and that of the therapist. Psychotherapy has to do with two people playing together. The corollary of this is that where playing is not possible, then the work done by the therapist is directed towards bringing the patient from a state of not being able to play to a state of being able to play.
>
> (1971:38)

In the UK, it was not until the 1980s that play therapy emerged as a different and distinct mode of working where play was the focus of the therapy rather than being used within psychotherapy or psychoanalysis. The Children's Hour trust initially taught professionals from various settings the basics of Axline's approach. However, it was the work of Sue Jennings and Ann Cattanach which brought play therapy into focus as a movement in its own right. They were both dramatherapists who incorporated aspects of non-directive play therapy into their practice which led to the Institute of Dramatherapy offering training in Play Therapy in 1990, and the setting up of the British Association of Play Therapists in 1992 (BAPT 2014). During this landmark year, three books were published, by West (*Child Centred Play Therapy*), McMahon (*The Handbook of Play Therapy*) and Wilson, Kendrick and Ryan (*Play Therapy: A Non-directive Approach for Children and Adolescents*); seminal texts which remain key reading for both those in training and practice today.

One of the cornerstones of non-directive play therapy is Jennings' Embodiment, Projection and Role (EPR) paradigm which charts the development of dramatic play from birth to seven years (1999). When children experience security and safety with their mother figure, their development follows a healthy trajectory and they are able to be playful and to play. Movement from embodied play through projective play and finally into role play is not an entirely linear process since children may move into the next aspect whilst retaining a foot in the previous or move forward and then need to return to an earlier stage. However, if progress is generally in a forward direction, then we would deem this to be a sign of good psychological well-being. Jennings notes that EPR is 'value free' since it does not rely on any particular psychological theory and so can be integrated into any psychological, therapeutic or educational practice. She has more recently developed the concept of Neuro-Dramatic-Play (NDP) which extends her original EPR thinking to include an exploration of the sensory experiences which occur between the mother figure and infant during pregnancy and the first months of life (2011).

Both Jennings and Cattanach continue to make significant contributions to the theory and practice of play therapy through their writings and across various training institutions. One important area of the practice of play therapy which Cattanach has addressed are the different settings in which we work as a result to changes in both society and approaches to mental health and well-being. Unlike the early psychoanalysts, many of us working as play therapists today do not work in the ideal clinical or office-based setting. We are more widely community based in schools, children's centres and specialist education settings such as pupil referral centres and special schools. We may work in more traditional settings such as Child and Adolescent Mental Health Services (CAMHS) and Children's Social Care (CSC) or we may work in family homes or in the outdoors. Cattanach recognizes not only the diversity of these work spaces and the clients we meet, but reminds us that since the training for play therapy is generally a postgraduate qualification, many play therapists will come from professions such as teaching, social work, psychology and nursing. As such, we need to be mindful of maintaining clarity about our differing roles if they are within the same organization, in order to avoid a conflict of interest which would be detrimental to the child and the work (Cattanach 2003). Above all, she stresses, the most important factor is to always maintain a safe therapeutic space where the child feels secure both physically and psychologically and can build trust and confidence in the relationship to hold them.

Changes in the structure of our society, the role of the family in children's lives, the economic and employment pressures on parents, and the increasing commercialization and sexualization of childhood all serve to influence the nature of the issues which clients bring to us. Contemporary edited collections by Prendiville and Howard (*Play Therapy Today* – 2014) and Le Vay and Cuschieri (*Challenges in the Theory and Practice of Play Therapy* – 2016) consider issues current in our practice such as interventions for children exposed to domestic violence, the role of neuroscience, therapist self-doubt, cultural challenges and research and play therapy.

Internationally, high quality training has been significant in raising the status of play therapy and play therapists, thus putting it on a professional footing. In the UK, Cattanach was fundamental in getting postgraduate training established at the University of Roehampton whilst Eileen Prendiville is Course Director at the Children's Therapy Centre in Ireland. Currently BAPT accredited training is offered through Roehampton and South Wales Universities with postgraduate qualifications available for both play therapy and therapeutic play skills. Although having links with Leeds Beckett University for its MA courses, Play Therapy UK (PTUK) is an independent organization that offers training in a range of therapeutic play skills as well as postgraduate play therapy qualifications. Both BAPT and PTUK as professional organizations maintain a register of accredited therapists overseen by the Professional Standards Authority.

Play Therapy Australia, established in 2001, reflects the international growth of interest in children's mental health and well-being and offers a training route for registration with the Australian Play Therapists Association (APTA). Accredited training is also offered in a number of other countries including Malaysia and Romania. This international perspective enriches play therapy and enhances our understanding of differing cultural attitudes and values. It gives us an opportunity to foster an attitude of co-operation rather than competition so that we can benefit from each other's experiences, acknowledging new developments as a chance to reflect on our own practice and where it may take us in the future.

There are undoubtedly other play therapists who have contributed to development of both theory and practice and whom I have not mentioned. They are not forgotten but are just beyond my sphere of experience for the moment. Just as I hope they will meet me through my writings, so I trust I will soon meet them too.

Thinking outside the box (of the playroom!)

Although here in the UK there are psychotherapists who have been working with adults in nature for many years from differing perspectives such as ecopsychology, ecotherapy, wild therapy and environmental arts therapy, working with nature is a much newer phenomenon in the world of play therapy. When I first started working outside, the only literature I had come across, which related specifically to play-based therapy with individual children, was Santostefano's book *Child Therapy in the Great Outdoors* (2004), Jordan and Marshall's work on holding the therapeutic frame in nature-based psychotherapy with adults (2010), which had been flagged up to me by a colleague, and there were books such as Louv's *Last Child in the Woods: Saving Our Children from Nature Deficit Disorder* (2005), Knight's *Forest School for All* (2011) and any number of books about outdoor learning in the early years. But, as we have seen in earlier discourse in this chapter, the traditional space for play therapy is viewed as the playroom, a secure and confidential place inside a building, or 'a box within a box within a box' (Chown 2014:139) and since Santostefano's book, no play therapist in the UK appears to have been writing about using outdoor spaces.

Santostefano wrote about his work with children in the therapeutic garden attached to his office. The garden had been specially designed to provide a range of natural features that might create opportunities for the enactment of embodied meanings and emotions. Coming from the relational psychoanalytic perspective, which suggests we are motivated not by biological drives, but rather by meaning given to our interactions, he describes how, in our first years of life, we create what he terms embodied life metaphors:

> as a child negotiates developmental needs and issues, the … [meanings given] to these experiences are constructed and expressed not with words but, rather, with non-verbal language that includes rhythms of gestures, facial expressions, tactile and kinaesthetic perceptions, actions, postures and emotional tones experienced by the child when interacting with others.
>
> (2004: 17)

He goes on to tell us that it is not only interactions with human others which contribute to our embodied life metaphors, but also interaction with 'nonhuman environments' which, he suggests, '*contain stimulation independent of the person interacting with it*' (p.18). So all our early interactions with both the people around us and the places we are in leave a lasting imprint on our minds and steer us towards future interactions and actions which allow us to recreate the 'feel' of our past traumas, thus inhibiting our ability to make and sustain fulfilling relationships. Therefore, in order to create new embodied life metaphors, which give us the opportunity to resolve earlier conflicts, we need to process these in active partnership with the therapist and in a range of locations, including the outdoors.

In an interview in 2012 with his publishers Jessica Kingsley, Dennis McCarthy, a psychotherapist currently working with both children and adults and specializing in sandplay, describes himself as having worked without any other template than '*a profound belief in the power of movement and play as both the language and medium of change*' (Jessica Kingsley Publishers 2012). This idea of working from our own experience and with our own beliefs resonates with my own pathway to working outdoors with nature. Whilst we might find some commonality in other theoretical perspectives and modes of working, we sometimes need to take a leap of faith, to step into the hitherto unknown and carve out a new path. McCarthy has developed an approach he calls 'dynamic' play therapy in which 'contained wildness' facilitates healthy development of the self and promotes a natural sense of self-regulation. Central to his work in the playroom is a deep sand box in which children can bury, sink or erupt either physically themselves or through their projective play with toys and objects. McCarthy has this to say of it:

> Having spent almost forty years watching children play in a deep sand box, and engaging with them in the experience, I can definitely say that the deep box is a much more visceral, emotional and energy-laden experience. When the child kneels down by the deep box, and digs their hand into the sand, there is an almost immediate, visible physical response.
>
> (2015:125)

It is this mind–body connection which is so much more fully utilized today than by the early psychotherapists who tended to work with the mind only. That children's experience has embodied meaning is critical to my own developing approach of play therapy in the outdoors. I like the idea of contained wildness but feel that it needs to be met by the uncontained wildness that nature can offer which, I believe, provides a more expansive, visceral and concrete metaphor with which children can 'play' creatively.

In their book *The Healing Forest in Post-Crisis Work with Children* (2013), Berger and Lahad, working in Israel, describe their nature therapy and expressive arts programme called 'A Safe Place'. Arising out of work following the Second Lebanon War, the programme aimed to provide a way of 'linking injury to nature – landscape, forests and wildlife' with the injury sustained by thousands of children in Northern Israel (p.16). Central to this programme was Berger's concept of nature therapy (2009), based on the assumption that nature is an independent space which belongs to neither therapist nor client and one which offers a therapeutic environment. Nature therapy considers us as not detached from our environment but interdependent with it so that we are both influenced by it and cast our own influence upon it. Including nature in the therapeutic process is to acknowledge her as an active partner with unique characteristics which the therapist can utilize to offer an enhanced experience of the therapeutic process. The dyadic relationship of traditional therapy becomes a triadic one with nature as the third partner in the process.

The therapeutic experience is also extended to include 'another' in animal-assisted therapy. In this developing mode of play therapy practice the integration of suitably trained animals such as dogs and horses again creates a third element or co-therapist with which and through which the client may relate within the therapeutic process. VanFleet (2016) notes that substantial research has clearly demonstrated the importance of the human–animal bond and the parallels between the behaviour children show to animals and to people. She stresses that animal-assisted play therapy focuses on the relationship with the animals and not control of them. Children learn to treat animals respectfully with tolerance and to recognize and respond to their feelings whilst developing a healthy and playful relationship with them. As we think of nature as the third element of the triadic therapeutic relationship, so it is with animals as part of nature – the non-human others we encounter.

My own work is still in its relative infancy and my thinking continues to develop. Whilst it incorporates aspects of the theories and concepts above, it is not derived from them. The theoretical underpinnings for and the pathway I have taken so far in establishing the approach I call Play Therapy in the Outdoors (PTITO) are detailed elsewhere in this book and in Chown (2014), but one of the key issues for me is establishing a much more democratic relationship with my clients than the one I feel often exists when they meet us in our playrooms. For in these rooms, we have chosen the toys and resources and have laid them out in a particular way. We may invite children into them, but they are still our rooms. Nature belongs to neither of us but also to both and for me that makes for a more equal relationship. Limits to ensure both physical and psychological safety and security are still necessary but working outside gives children the opportunity to take the lead much more fully as the case study below illustrates.

As a result of a recent accident, my capacity for rapid movement over uneven ground has been slightly reduced. This is not in a way that compromises the safety of clients, but means I have to take a little more care outside. The children I work with know this because it also means sitting on the floor with them can be tricky. They accept this, usually without question and we play together without a problem.

Jason is seven years old. He lives with his Dad and brother but wants to live with his Mum and is full of angry feelings. He spends little time in the classroom but is supported in a nurture room by 'his' support assistants, one in the morning and the other in the afternoon. He has two, because on some days he is exhausting to be with.

He and I have been working together for ten months and he has been very controlling and directive. He has recently started to access the outdoor areas beyond the playroom. On one occasion he wanted to take me into the woods, right at the back where there is a pathway which can be tricky to negotiate since it is a little overgrown and rough underfoot. As we walked out I reminded him that I might not be able to go as fast as him because of my 'poorly' knee. He simply replied 'OK' and off we went with him leading the way as we had not used that area of the woods together before.

When we got there, Jason took charge. He indicated tree stumps and large stones I might trip over, he held back low branches and brambles, aware that although he might pass under them, I was much taller and could not. He waited if I was lagging behind and he reassured me that we were 'nearly at the proper path' when he thought I might be wondering how much further we had to go. In short, he showed great care towards me, something he had not done before or perhaps had not felt able to do because we were in the playroom.

Since our playroom is one that is used for other activities for the rest of the week, there is an implied ownership by the school – it is a school space, and although the woods are in the school grounds, the children seem to see them as theirs, because they are beyond the borders of the buildings. It was this that enabled him to take on a new role within our relationship; to equal it and extend the care he did not receive at home to another, to experience it for himself and to experience being in charge in a positive rather than overtly controlling way. Since then, we have spent several sessions outside and the nature of our relationship has changed. It is much more of a partnership now and we engage in co-constructed play activities, at Jason's request – he has invited me into his play, is working at a much deeper level and is beginning to find his own 'voice' can be other than the very angry boy.

Fearn (2014), in discussing working therapeutically in the outdoors, notes that 'The natural world exists in community: rocks, streams, soil, plants, trees and living creatures living off and with each other in synchronised, reciprocal arrangements that have evolved over many generations … these are elemental places where children can play naturally' (2014:116). How much richer a sensory environment this sounds than the words 'the playroom'! And the rhythms of nature are important to us as human beings, the rhythm of our bodies – heartbeat, blood flow and breath; birth, life and death; the rhythm of the turning year – spring, summer, autumn and winter; planting, tending and harvest; and the rhythm of our relationships – the to and fro, one to another and back again. They are living and vital, we 'feel' them with all of our senses, they are visceral and ever changing. These rhythms have crossed time and land-scapes, have formed a pathway from one generation to the next to the next and carried human and non-human life forms to where we are today. As society advances technologically it is all too easy for us to lose touch with what is real – to enter the virtual reality where we can exist in isolation from others while maintaining an illusion that we are being sociable – to exist in our minds but not in our bodies. The early psychoanalysts treated the mind and saw the body as separate. Later, the integration between the two was recognized and a third element added to give us the mind–body–spirit connection. Now, because of the technological revolution and our disconnection from nature, we need more than ever to hold this clearly in our mind and look to the 'nature mother' to pro-vide a way of us nourishing all three. Nowhere is this more crucial than in our work as play therapists. Satish Kumar, co-founder of the Schumacher College and international peace and environment activist, writes about how there needs to be a new trinity for our times, that of 'soil, soul and society' (2013). This, I think, parallels the process we as therapists are engaged in with our clients when we work in outdoor spaces. Through a multifaceted connection with the soil, we can heal the soul and enable a healthier connection with society, both in interpersonal and intrapersonal relationships. It is powerful stuff!

References

Association for Play Therapy (2016) *About APT.* Available from: www.a4pt.org/page/AboutAPT [Accessed 27th December 2016]

Axline, V. (1964) *Dibs in Search of Self.* USA: Pelican Books

Axline, V. (1969) *Play Therapy.* Canada: Ballantyne Books

Berger, R. (2009) *Nature Therapy – Developing a Framework for Practice.* Available from: www.naturetherapy.org.il/index.php?option=com_content&view=article&id=188&Itemid=37&lang=en [Accessed 14th October 2016]

Berger, R. and Lahad, M. (2013) *The Healing Forest in Post-Crisis Work with Children: A Nature Therapy and Expressive Arts Programme for Groups.* London: Jessica Kingsley Publishers

British Association of Play Therapists (2013) *A History of Play Therapy.* Available from: www.bapt.info/play-therapy/history-play-therapy/ [Accessed 14th December 2016]

Cattanach, A. (2003) *Introduction to Play Therapy.* Hove: Brunner–Routledge

Center for Play Therapy (no date) *Meet Our Founder – Founder and Director Emeritus.* Available from: http://cpt.unt.edu/about-us/meet-our-founder [Accessed 7th December 2016]

Chown, A. (2014) *Play Therapy in the Outdoors: Taking Play Therapy out of the Playroom and into Natural Environments.* London: Jessica Kingsley Publishers

Farleigh Dickinson University (2006) About the Author. *FDU Magazine Online* Winter/Spring 2006, no page number. Available from: www.fdu.edu/newspubs/magazine/06ws/schaefer.htmlrapy.org.uk/Training [Accessed 13th December 2016]

Fearn, M. (2014) Working therapeutically in the outdoors. In Prendiville, E. and Howard, J. (eds) *Play Therapy Today: Contemporary Practice with Individuals, Groups and Carers.* Oxford: Routledge

Friedman, H. and Rogers Mitchell, R. (2005) *What is Sandplay?* Available from: www.sandplay.org/about-sandplay/what-is-sandplay/ [Accessed 3rd January 2017]

Homeyer, L. E. and Sweeney, D. S. (2017) *Sandtray Therapy: A Practical Manual* (3rd edition). New York: Routledge

Jennings, S. (1999) *An Introduction to Developmental Play Therapy.* London: Jessica Kingsley Publishers

Jennings, S. (2011) *Healthy Attachments and Neuro-Dramatic-Play.* London: Jessica Kingsley Publishers

Jessica Kingsley Publishers (2012) *Helping Things Fall Apart, The Paradox of Play – An Interview with Dennis McCarthy (Part 1).* [Blog Post] Available from: www.jkp.com/jkpblog/2012/02/interview-dennis-mccarthy-a-manual-of-dynamic-play-therapy-part-one/ [Accessed 12th December 2016]

Jordan, M. and Marshall, H. (2010) Taking counselling and psychotherapy outside: Destruction or enrichment of the therapeutic frame? *European Journal of Psychotherapy and Counselling* 12 (4), 345–359

Knight, S. (2011) *Forest School for All.* London: Sage

Kumar, S. (2013) *Soil, Soul, Society: A New Trinity for Our Time.* Sussex: Leaping Hare Press

Landreth, G. (2002) *Play Therapy: The Art of the Relationship* (2nd edition). Hove: Brunner–Routledge

Le Vay, D. and Cuschieri, E. (eds) (2016) *Challenges in the Theory and Practice of Play Therapy.* Oxon: Routledge

Louv, R. (2005) *Last Child in the Woods: Saving Our Children from Nature Deficit Disorder.* London: Atlantic Books

lowenfeld.org (no date) *Dr Margaret Lowenfeld (1890–1973).* Available from: http://lowenfeld.org/aboutlowenfeld.html [Accessed 3rd December 2016]

Maslow, A. (1943) A theory of human motivation. *Psychological Review* 50 (4), 370–396. Available from: doi:10.1037/h0054346 [Accessed 23rd September 2016]

McCarthy, D. (2015) *Deep Play: Exploring the Use of Depth in Psychotherapy with Children.* London: Jessica Kingsley Publishers

McMahon, L. (1992) *The Handbook of Play Therapy.* London: Routledge

Moustakas, C. (1973) *Children in Play Therapy.* USA: Jason Aronson

Prendiville, E. and Howard, J. (eds) (2014) *Play Therapy Today: Contemporary Practice with Individuals, Groups and Carers.* Oxon: Routledge

Rowan, J. (2005) *A Guide to Humanistic Psychology* (3rd edition). Available from: http://ahpp.org.uk/humanistic-psychology/ [Accessed 14th December 2016]

Santostefano, S. (2004) *Child Therapy in the Great Outdoors: A Relational View.* Jersey: The Analytic Press

Science Museum (no date) *Toys used for Lowenfeld's 'World Technique' therapy, London, England, 1920–1970.* Available from: www.sciencemuseum.org.uk/broughttolife/objects/display?id=93414&image=10 [Accessed 12th December 2016]

United States Department of Agriculture (no date) *Differences between Coaching, Counseling, Managing, Mentoring, Consulting and Training*. Available from: www.dm.usda.gov/employ/vu/coaching-diff.htm [Accessed 6th December 2016]

VanFleet, R. (2016) *About the Playful Pooch Program*. Available from: http://play-therapy.com/playfulpooch/about.html#over [Accessed 23rd January 2017]

West, J. (1992) *Child Centred Play Therapy* (2nd edition). London: Arnold

Wilson, K., Kendrick, P. and Ryan, V. (1992) *Play Therapy: A Non-directive Approach for Children and Adolescents*. London: Bailliere and Tindall

Winnicott, D. (1971) *Playing and Reality*. East Sussex: Brunner–Routledge

Chapter 2

Considering the concept and purpose of play

> Play may be defined as activity, which may be physical or mental, existing apparently for its own sake or having for the individual as its main aim, the pleasure which the activity itself yields.
>
> (Chown 1963)

In considering the concept or process of play, it might at first appear important to try to define it. Sutton-Smith (1997:9) suggests, however, that there is much ambiguity and very little agreement amongst us when we try to determine the nature of play and playing. He notes that in thinking about play, *'our implicit narratives or "rhetorics" ... are part of multiple broad symbolic systems – political, religious, social, and educational – through which we construct the meaning of the culture within which we live'*. So it would seem that play may be a much more complex activity than it at first appears and not only the province of babies and children, but also, in differing forms, the activities of adolescents and adults. Perhaps, in trying to define such complexity, we are in danger of losing much of the process and becoming instead too sharply focused on the function and purpose of the play rather than on the intrinsic value of a free-flowing and unfettered process which comes from within the individual and which may, at any one time, be about nothing in particular and everything personal. This is underlined by the core principles of playwork, which state that *'for playworkers, it is the process that takes precedence, a process which is determined and controlled by the child and which follows their own ideas, interests and instincts for their own reason'* (Playwork Principles Scrutiny Group 2015).

Research from the University of Gloucester (Lester and Russell 2008:2) which considered the nature of play found that while there was disagreement on a precise definition, there were a number of common characteristics found in the literature studies which included the ideas of play being:

- based on a sense of free will and control, either individually or within the group
- flexible and adaptive, using objects and rules in a variety of changing ways
- non-literal, 'as if' behaviour – it can rearrange or turn the world upside down
- unpredictable, spontaneous, innovative and creative

All of these are key aspects of the process of play therapy which incorporates Jennings' (1999) idea that a healthy developmental trajectory involves children in three core aspects of dramatic play – Embodiment, Projection and Role (EPR). Play therapy sessions are child directed within the context of a safe, secure and predictable relationship that recognizes the need for minimal limits and boundaries. The toys and resources are used symbolically by the child so that what they represent may change with each client. The ability to play 'as if' is crucial since it enables children to take on the role of another and to understand how it might feel to be them and this, Jennings suggests, is how empathy develops. The play children engage in during play therapy is by its very nature unpredictable, spontaneous, innovative and creative because it arises from within the child and in the moment of the action itself. Although the EPR paradigm can seem to present as a linear model, children do not pass along it smoothly moving neatly from one 'stage' to the next. As with other linear models which are referred to later in this chapter, movement through them can involve stepping into the next stage before the former is completed so there is an overlap and even an occasional leap ahead when a later stage might be entered briefly before there is a retreat to the earlier stage.

Sutton-Smith (1997) highlights this when he suggests that the idea that both play and development are a set of stages which children pass through and that there is a distinct relationship between the two – that play leads development – is a somewhat flawed theory. He considers that the increase in positive developmental outcomes after what he describes as play training has taken place, is as likely as not to be due to the new, more focused relationship with the teacher (or other adult), a suggestion which resonates clearly with the idea of the therapeutic alliance developed between the play therapist and her client.

Despite this suggestion that play may not necessarily lead to development, the belief that playing is a crucial aspect of all areas of children's development is widely held in current educational thinking and echoed in the theories which underpin play therapy practice. However, Sutton-Smith's idea that neither play nor development happen in fixed and defined stages is helpful to our understanding of the nature of children's play and in aiding us to keep in mind the idea that play exists for its own sake and that to expect a particular outcome at a particular point is to narrow both the focus and definition. Since the approach outlined in this book is a synthesis of both therapeutic and educational thinking, the stance it takes is that through play, children learn about their world, their place in it and their potential as an individual in interactions with it, both on an interpersonal and intrapersonal level. In this respect, their world includes both the physical environment and the relationships they make both with it and with the others in it.

In attempting to define play and its part in children's development we may consider various theoretical perspectives which suggest a staged model such as those of Freud, Erikson and Piaget (see McMahon 1992:4) but accept that even if there are a series of stages through which we might pass, as with the EPR paradigm, we do not travel along a coherent, systematic, one-stage-after-another pathway. Rather we meander, sometimes moving forward, sometimes back, sometimes wandering off on a side path and sometimes staying still to consolidate and consider. Watch children's undirected play, and this is self-evident. They do not generally conform to patterns of our adult making. They create their own reality which can appear to those watching to be chaotic, rumbustious and without purpose, but through this process, their own patterns are established and learning and development happen, even within that whirlwind space. As adults we are not necessarily privy to exactly what they have mastered as a result or even if they have.

Consider two boys, one aged four, the other nearly seven, engaged in a game of 'scrumbly puddings' in which they wrap themselves in their duvets, fall down on top of each other and then come to 'get' the adults in the room all the while shouting 'here comes the scrumbly pudding' and shrieking loudly with delight! We might assume that there was some learning going on, perhaps about physical strength from their tussles on the floor, perhaps some idea of how to elicit certain reactions from adults as a result of their 'attacks' on them or a reminder of what it felt like to feel safely cocooned in a soft space, all of which may be true. But perhaps what they learned was simply the sheer, exhilarating joy of being; of feeling free to roll and tumble and shout, of being protected by a soft layer to cushion any falls and the feeling of being a child playing with no purpose other than for the pleasure of the play itself. In the outcome driven, results laden, performance management culture of today, we have perhaps forgotten the concept of 'joy', a somewhat underused word describing a state of blissful, delightful, thrilling ecstatic pleasure – pleasure for pleasure's sake.

We do of course need to be mindful of theory and use it to underpin our thinking for without it our work becomes free-floating, without the anchorage that grounds the work in the reality of being a child. But in that 'being a child', we must remember that rarely do we conform to either perceived and expected norms, or the expectations of those around us.

Within the traditions of play therapy we can come upon a tension arising from being informed by theory but also bound or constrained by it when as Robertson (2016) tells us, '*theoretical models don't make sense of a child's experience … we don't always need to understand or know [why]*'. When we meet children in play therapy, we are very much in the present with them and to live in the present is dynamic and also the place where new theory can be generated. The processes we are part of today are tomorrow's theories. So if when we are with our clients, we are so concerned with which theoretical perspective we should be working from, then we are not truly present for them and neither are we likely to be aware of the potential of the moment to show us that something different may be needed, something which has not necessarily gone before.

The Scottish Government paper 'Pre Birth to Three – Positive Outcomes for Scotland's Children and Families' (Learning and Teaching Scotland (LTS) 2010), like Sutton-Smith, recognizes that there has been continuing and wide-ranging debate about the definition of play and its purpose. It notes that the main contributors to pedagogic discussion, particularly within early years' education communities, have been theorists such as Vygotsky, Bruner, Montessori and Froebel who have contributed much to education thinking in recent times. To this list we might add Loris Malaguzzi, whose work has given rise to the Reggio Emilia approach popular in early years settings, and also highlight the Danish Forest School movement whose particular promotion of the importance of outdoor play has had a wide impact in the UK in the last two decades. All of these place the idea of social learning from the community at their heart, whether that community be family, school group or those within the town where you live. LTS goes on to note:

> These frameworks can widen thinking and help to ensure that research impacts on practice through creating play environments that are meaningful and appropriate to children's development. There is a strong correlation between children's learning through play in the earliest years and the impact in later life. Therefore, the importance of play cannot be overstated.
>
> (p.71)

It further highlights play as enabling children to:

- make important connections so that they can make sense of their world
- consolidate and celebrate what they know and can do
- act out and process day-to-day experiences
- thrive, develop self-confidence and social skills
- experiment with and manage feelings

(p.72)

(It is interesting to note that there is no reference here to 'meet predetermined aims, objectives and targets'!)

Brown and Patte (2013) consider play as benefitting children across five domains: cognitive, creative, emotional, physical and social, and recognize from their review of research which compares play to work, that for children, play is not work. That is to say children see a distinct difference between play and work, with play involving choice and direction, and work being directed by teachers (or other adults) as not being play, even where there are attempts to disguise it as such.

So there is broad agreement that play has a significant role in children's development and in their learning. Furthermore, any definition of play must include recognition that for it to be beneficial, it needs to be in the hands of the children themselves, emanating from within them and from the interactions they have with the environment around them, but in the context of their total learning environment which includes adults. What we need to guard against however is becoming the dominant factor in their play, guiding it to suit our ends and using it as a means to create frameworks with fixed expectations of how they will perform.

Early developmental play

> A human life develops from the delicate interplay of nature and nurture, the meeting of a bundle of inherited potentials and the cultural, social and personal influences of the adults in an infant's life.
>
> (Music 2011:24)

In addition to incorporating the EPR paradigm, play therapy is underpinned by the attachment theory of John Bowlby which informs two key aspects of the therapeutic process. The first is the idea of the therapeutic alliance – the relationship between the client and therapist. This involves the focused, attentive and attuned adult who is present only for the child, providing a reliable model of positive attachment; of how an adult can be non-judgemental, accepting and nurturing. The second is that of the relationships which the child has in their own world and how these may have impacted on them. If they have been held in the mind of significant others, attended to with care and sensitivity and have been given unconditional positive regard, they will grow up with a positive sense of self, an understanding of who they are and that they are important to others. If they have not received this nurturing care and responsive attuned attention, they may grow to see themselves as unlovable and unloved. Our sense of self as a person is developed through these relationships, is a reflection of how we are seen and thought of by those around us and so is socially constructed and dependent on others. In other words, it is co-constructed just as the play in play therapy is co-constructed, arising from both the child and the therapist; from the therapeutic relationship they develop and the environment in which the play takes place.

In early attachment relationships in the Western world, there tend to be two players, the mother or mother figure and the infant. In considering at what point this relationship begins, we need to look prenatally to see the influence of both nature and nurture. Music (2011:14) reminds us that not only is the foetus *its own being, with its own rhythms, urges and biological expectations* but that it can also control its very unique intrauterine environment by such means as the position it lies in and determining when birth will occur. It also has the capacity to respond to stimuli such as music and rhythm and to the mother's state of mind. It is able to promote a kind of early dance of physical attunement through actions such as triggering an increase in nutrients it needs by sending hormones into the mother's bloodstream to raise her blood pressure. This in turn causes a response in the mother's body and so even before birth, a 'to and fro' rhythm of interaction is developing. Jennings (2011:13) considers the womb to provide a *'whole sensory system: temperature, sound, rhythm, touch and emotional changes of mood and energy'* and also recognizes the profound effect of the mother's sensory experiences on the well-being of the infant, noting how these can influence the developing in-utero relationship between them. And so pregnancy which at first might appear to be a biologically based process can be seen to also have psychological and social influences. Jennings also suggests that this early interaction with the mother figure from within the containment of the 'safe waters' of the womb, is at the core of a set of primary circles of containment, care and attachment which form the basis of Neuro-Dramatic-Play (NDP). These dramatic and playful interactions take place in the period before birth and in the early months after and overlap with the idea of EPR development from birth to seven years.

Winnicott (1971) referred to the space between the mother figure and the child where the first postnatal playful interactions occur as the intermediate playground. It is in this space, which is replicated by the therapeutic alliance between the child and therapist, that playfulness can develop. The circle of care formed by the mother's body and by her holding of the child, creates feelings of containment: of safety and security. The interactions between the infant and the mother figure, whilst seemingly based on physical care, create opportunities for playful responses from both.

What neuroscience tells us

Research during the 1980s led neuroscientists to the discovery of mirror neurons which they believed showed that humans are able to imitate another from the first few hours after birth, far earlier than it had been thought to happen. This imitation implied learning since it appeared that the observer transformed the action they were seeing into one they completed themselves and which could be either similar or identical to the first action. Rizzolatti (2005) suggests this process was composed of two related cognitive phenomena: firstly, the capacity to make sense of others' actions, and secondly, to replicate this once it is understood. This then suggested new meaning for those early facial expressions of babies once thought to be of a more biological origin, since it was now felt that they had an innate capacity to imitate the expressions and actions of the mother figure. Research by Zeedyk at the University of Dundee, Scotland and released on the DVD 'The Connected

Baby' (2011) further evidenced the idea that babies are born with the capacity to communicate and connect emotionally with others. The film showed babies responding to the rhythms, vocal tones and movements of their parents, grandparents and siblings in what Zeedyk described as 'emotional exchanges'. However, more recent research conducted by Slaughter and her colleagues from the Early Cognitive Development Centre at the University of Queensland now suggests that imitation is not innate but is learned in the first months of an infant's life, possibly by watching others imitate them, since they also found that parents imitate their babies around once every two minutes (Cell Press 2016). Curiously, this 'does it, doesn't it' back and forth outcome from research regarding the innate potential of infants to imitate almost mirrors the interactions they are studying.

Whether we have the innate capacity to imitate from birth, or acquire it in the first few months through interactions with others, it is a remarkable process and Glasgow Koste puts in a plea for us to recognize the significance of it to the human condition and to restore it to its rightful and essential place in our thinking:

> To imitate, 'to hold the mirror up to nature' requires, after all, a complex operation beginning with the child's selective observation of the world around and within himself, melding into the absorption of this data, a recombining and interpreting of it, and a *reproduction* of some new arrangement of it.
>
> (1995:14, original emphasis)

Whilst there may remain a difference in views about the potential for imitation from our earliest postnatal moments, these first playful interactions between the infant and the mother figure establish the to and fro rhythm of turn-taking which is the pre-requisite for the development of language and conversation. In these interactions, we are not merely responding to another, communicating our conscious awareness, but are seeking the self in the other, demonstrating intent (Trevarthan 2004).

Because we are pre-verbal, our connections to others are embodied, held within our physical being and have embodied meaning. However, they establish both physical and psychological reactions which form the pattern of relationship initially between the infant and the mother figure but which we carry with us into the future. Siegal (2011) tells us that in these early stages when the pattern for our future relationships is being laid down, the most important aspect of parenting is not the doing, but the being with, since our most important infant experience is of being joined with another. This idea of a unity between two occurs when our mother figure is fully attuned to us, caught up in the act of connecting with our subjective self and *being* in the present with us rather than concerned with *doing* something for us. Siegal describes the neurobiology behind this as the left hemisphere of the brain looking outward to the exterior world, concerned with language and the detail of problem solving and social display rules, whilst the right hemisphere is concerned with our interior subjective experience, the context and the connection with the interior world of others. Simply put, he suggests that babies therefore search the world with their right hand but self-soothe with their left.

Siegal also notes that our early care experiences structure what he calls our synaptic architecture which not only connects our left and right hemispheres across the corpus callosum allowing for communication between different parts of the brain, but also extends 'downwards' into our body, to give us the feeling of 'being'. When our early experiences are positive, we feel connected but when they are neglectful or abusive, we experience feelings of disconnection, from both our self and others. In this unintegrated state, our feelings become intolerable and threaten to overwhelm us. When our very survival is compromised, our responses are triggered in what we tend to think of as our primitive brain, the amygdala, with our physiological responses being controlled by the brain stem within it. These visceral responses to stress include increased heart rate to pump blood to our muscles and other vital organs, changes in body temperature and rapid breathing designed to increase oxygen to the brain and so increase alertness. In this aroused state we are prepared to fight or flee or, in some cases, freeze or dissociate ourselves from the event. When this happens, we are unable to access the functions of our neo-cortex responsible for higher order thinking, reasoning, decision making and conscious experience since our body is on 'automatic pilot' to survive the event that is occurring. If the cause of our stress or fear is persistent, our baseline state of arousal is altered to such an extent that our responses remain highly reactive and survival oriented impacting on the making and sustaining of meaningful future relationships, as Bloom notes: 'The nature of the relationship between an infant and its primary caregivers underlies the development of the psyche throughout later life. Even the primordial memory of intra-uterine life has been shown to affect both body and psyche after birth' (2006:4).

Bloom sees embodiment as involving three aspects of self – emotional, mental and sensory – which are contained within the very structure of the body but responsive to both internal and external stimuli, and Totton tells us that '*The human body is not something that exists on its own, in isolation ... it needs others for its well-being in very fundamental ways ... we form relationships through and as our bodies*' (2003:25). Our early experiences of being cared for, of being held and stroked, soothed and patted, massaged and comforted, in short of being attended to and affirmed as a loved and valued being, create a positive sense of 'body self', our sense of being alive, of having substance and of being connected. If our early care is lacking in warmth and affection, and our basic needs are not reliably met or we are abused in some other way, then we may grow to have a distorted view of our body or no real sense of it at all. In this way, we can be said to '*inhabit a cold, flat two-dimensional body rather than one that is warm, pulsating, rhythmic and alive to the experiences created by, with and through 'others' in our lives'* (Chown 2014:95).

The 'where' and 'how' of play

So, in our early months, play arises out of the playful exchanges between the infant and the mother figure with the body itself as the object of the play in a kind of practice play where the infant repeats motor actions that are the cause of interesting events (Garner and Bergen 2006). As we develop and grow, our physical world expands and our physical capabilities change so that we move from lying to crawling and sitting and then to standing and toddling and finally to walking. How we view our physicality and understand our body and its capacity for movement arises out of our early explorations of both our physical space and the objects in it. Throughout this time, we are playing, using toys and objects as well as the growing number of people and places in our lives. Play enables us to learn how to master this new and ever expanding universe of experiences.

Projective play with toys and objects external to ourselves gives rise to the development of symbolic or pretend play where we can utilize these as something other than for their original purpose so that a plastic bowl might become a hat or a box may be worn as a shoe. Garner and Bergen (2006) suggest that although pretend play may appear in the latter part of the first year, it is generally solitary and focused on the self in activities that reflect everyday occurrences such as washing and cleaning teeth. It is not until after the first twelve months that social pretend play develops as part of a more typical pattern where pretend towards self is followed by pretend towards objects with persona such as teddies and dolls and finally social pretend involving others. As play progresses, so too do the other domains of cognition, language, socialization and physicality. Garner and Bergen argue that it is again difficult to determine which gives rise to the other *'whether play causes developmental changes or whether other developmental changes cause changes in play'* (2006:10). They conclude that this reflects the debate around nature versus nurture and that we are perhaps best placed not to concern ourselves about which comes first but rather give time for exploration of the nature of both and how they might interact to enhance each other. Out of social pretend play comes role play when we try out or rehearse our understanding of what it is like to be 'as if' – to be another being or thing, or to exist in another world. We might pretend to be someone we have contact with every day, a superhero or a character from a book or TV programme and exist in a transformed everyday world or an imagined one where we are in charge and have power.

From the age of four onwards, children's physicality develops and, as their world expands, they occupy more space, running, jumping, dancing, climbing and beginning to use outdoor toys such as climbing frames, slides, trikes, bikes and scooters. They take delight in their bodies and all that they can do. At this point in their development, they are likely to be aware of the bio-logical differences between boys and girls and may also start to be influenced by the others in their lives. Children who have had positive early nurtur-ing relationships with secure attachments to their primary carers develop a sense of an autonomous self, of being able to take action by themselves, for themselves and with their own self. This will have come about through the knowledge that their mother figure has identified so strongly with them as a baby that it feels as if they are one being, that the infant's needs are her needs. Being the centre of focus for the mother figure gives the infant feel-ings of omnipotence and power. If the infant were to remain in this state into later life, it would be detrimental to both their emotional well-being and the relationships they might make since omnipotence in the real grown-up world is very destructive, particularly in relationships with others. Typically, as that first relationship develops, the infant grows to see that she is separate from the mother figure, can exist beyond her and that they each have their own emotional experiences. It is now that the co-constructed relationship strengthens and there is action and reaction giving rise to the interaction which enables healthy individuation and the beginnings of the independent, autonomous self.

This experience of a positive attachment to the primary carer provides us with what Bowlby (1988) termed the 'secure base', that which we can move away from knowing we are held in mind. We need this secure base, cou-pled with a strong sense of our body self and the knowledge that we can be autonomous, for our developing play is risky; physically, emotionally and socially and it can also be cognitively challenging. Jennings (2011) suggests that our first experience of risk comes in the early physically collaborative interactions we have with the mother figure such as rocking, bouncing and singing. She explains how these early experiences contain the dual compo-nents of both risk and ritual. Because we feel safe in the containment of our mother figure's arms, we can take a risk with the danger of being bounced or swung gently upwards and, equally importantly, enjoy the thrilling feeling that creates within us. As we become more independent and autonomous, we take a risk when we move away from our primary attachment figure and as we grow and move farther afield, increasing the range of movements we can make and actions we take, there is risk in what we do, how we do it and where these activities take place.

Embodied developmental trauma

Having the experience of a reliable and consistent pattern of care, affirming attention and playful, dramatic, physical and sensory interactions gives us a positive sense of our body self, an understanding of how it *feels* to be 'me' and prepares us well to face the challenges and risks involved in living a fulfill-ing life and experiencing mutually satisfying relationships. But what of those infants whose early experiences gave rise not to feelings of security, safety and containment but of fear, anxiety, discomfort, distress and even terror – the fear of utter annihilation? Then, how it feels to be 'me' is frightening, overwhelming and impossible to bear. The infant who has experienced a secure attachment to their mother figure through her attuned and reciprocal physical and verbal communications will be able to tolerate distress, knowing that she will understand the proximity seeking behaviours and responses and have the capacity to soothe and calm so that the infant learns how to self-regulate. But when this level of attunement has been absent from the parenting received, the infant will have no mechanisms for affect regulation and their capacity to tolerate both pleasant and unpleasant feelings will be at least minimal or even non-existent (Ogden et al. 2006).

Children who have experienced this kind of 'developmental trauma' (Van der Kolk 2015) will have no awareness of the connection between the bodily sensations they are experiencing in the here and now and past trauma. Because these early, pre-verbal experiences are embodied – held within us – they give rise to behaviours and feelings which can interfere with daily life, inhibit mutually satisfying relationships and leave us feeling psychologically and physically unsafe. Aiyegbusi (2004:53) suggests that *'for a person who does not feel they have been loved for the person they are, or feels that no interest or value has been paid to their mind or what they think about'* it is entirely possible that they come to see themselves as 'body' alone. This focus on the physical self as separate from the affective and cognitive self is even more likely where there has been physical or sexual abuse or neglect and gives rise to use of the body to communicate what it is difficult or impossible to articulate with words. In many cases, this leads to responses to others which are aggressive, either physically, verbally, emotionally or all three together. Nowhere was this more obvious than in my own work with boys who had been excluded from school and who *'paradoxically use(d) their bodies aggressively but in defence of a very fragile sense of self, as a result of … negative emotions such as shame, guilt, anger, anxiety, inadequacy and frustration'* (Chown 2015:49). With this form of physical communication where emotions are activated but fail to guide effective action, there is no recognition of what is being felt or what the meaning of that feeling is. Van der Kolk (2006:xxi) notes:

> [An] inability to recognize what is going on inside – to correctly identify sensations, emotions and physical states – causes individuals to be out of touch with their needs and to be incapable of taking care of them, and often extends to having difficulty appreciating the emotional states and needs of those around them.

In adulthood, those who have developed secure attachments during infancy, demonstrate congruent behaviour where physical movements match inner affect states and promote effective action appropriate to the experience or situation. They are comfortable with themselves whether engaged in autonomous actions or needing help and support.

Ogden et al. (2006) give us a comprehensive description of the relationship between attachment styles and their corresponding bodily states. They note that those infants whose mother figure appears to withdraw from them or repel their physical contact, effectively blocking the proximity seeking behaviours, leave the child with an insecure and avoidant style of attachment. This then manifests itself as movements which are defensive in nature, awkward, stiff or passively withdrawn. There would be a lack of emotional expression and eye contact and a low level of arousal. Infants who have developed insecure ambivalent attachments demonstrate physical movements which are more likely to be directed towards a discharge of high arousal than towards purposeful actions to gain proximity to the mother figure. Behaviour appears dysregulated, agitated and vocalized even though there may be a greater sense of congruency between internal states and external movement. Those infants who have developed disorganized or disoriented attachments as a result of a mother figure who has been frightening or frightened, maintain a hyper or hypo-regulated state for lengthy periods of time and may appear frozen, unduly aggressive or chaotic reflecting the freeze, fight or flight response triggered deep within the oldest part of our brains.

Discussing this level of developmental trauma, Van der Kolk (2015) notes how children who do not feel safe and whose behaviours are symptomatic of being scared to death or fighting for their very survival are often diagnosed with disorders such as anxiety, reactive attachment disorder (RAD), oppositional defiance disorder (ODD), attention deficit and hyperactivity disorder (ADHD) or post traumatic stress disorder (PTSD). He suggests, however, that none of these diagnoses is helpful to our understanding of the root of the behaviours; that the child does not trust that either her mother figure or any other adult can help her or keep her safe. He sees such diagnoses as emphasizing behaviour control rather than recognizing that such behaviours arise from interpersonal trauma with the long-term effects of such devastating early experiences including difficulties with emotional regulation, attention and concentration, impulse control and self and relational schemas.

Many of the interventions or treatments such children will be subject to within medical, social and educational systems will involve strategies to change behaviour, improve parenting and develop more secure attachments between the primary carers and the child. While each of these have a place, they can appear to be akin to a topical dressing – a sticking plaster – in that they do not really get under the skin of the problem to the heart of the matter, that the child has been traumatized. Interestingly, both of these expressions relate so directly to our physicality that they surely tell us that without involving the child's sense of body self in the process, the embodied trauma will not be resolved on a more permanent basis. Since the trauma is encoded in the body as procedural memories, an active, physical means of processing them is needed. Such activity is more likely in an outdoor setting where there is a much bigger yet still contained space that allows for more expansive movement and a deeper sensory connection.

Lost for words

One of the common aspects of therapeutic interventions is generally the processing of trauma through the creation of a narrative which helps to differentiate between past and present so that we can locate the traumatic experiences in the past, and understand that though danger was present then, we are safe in the here and now. However, this requires us to have an understanding of both timescale and perspective, controlled by areas of the brain which often shut down as the trauma is lived. When this happens, we experience the event not coherently as a story with beginning, middle and end but as a frightening series of emotions, images, smells, sounds and perhaps even tastes. To be truly therapeutic, these *bodily sensations* need processing which in traditional talking therapy requires us to be able to describe them, to put words to feelings which are so overwhelming that they continue to terrify us to the extent that we lose our capacity to recognize them. The inability to do this is known as alexithymia, and completely disables us from correctly identifying sensations, emotions and physical states (Van der Kolk 2006). For children, this verbalization is an even more monumental task since the development of their language may not be sufficient for them to have ever learned the words for the more usual emotions experienced, hence the appropriateness of play therapy, where the 'narrative' is told symbolically and through metaphor and so does not rely on language at all.

Issues of transference

Embodiment or sensory play during the traditional play therapy process provides opportunities for a new, more positive and integrated sense of body self. However, where this is absent or distorted, I believe a much more real and visceral sensory experience is needed and one which I have found cannot be provided by the playroom alone. One aspect of the playroom which mitigates against this is the extent to which it can be physically challenging. This statement may appear to be somewhat contradictory when all our instincts, training and ethical guidelines tell us client safety, both physical and psychological, must be at the heart of our work. But children's 'free' play is characterized in part by its expansive nature. They run and jump, shout and bellow, whirl and dance and make big movements. Although some playrooms may be large enough to accommodate such activity, expansive noise and movement can seem overwhelming for both child and therapist in a smaller space, a feeling which might replicate those experienced at the time of the original trauma. Whilst the therapist will be able to sit with the feeling of being overwhelmed, it may be too great for the child and rather than increasing their capacity to tolerate distress, may lead to further disintegration. Outside, these feelings can be discharged in a way that allows for some temporary escape until the child has a more robust sense of their body self to know that they are not going to be crushed by what they are feeling. A play therapist colleague working with looked after children gave the following description of just such an expansive activity:

> She needed to make an enormous mess (contained in a huge black square tray), for which the outdoors was ideal, as there were no walls to splatter! Then, when she moved to mainly role play, she created a really colourful 'stage', using long lengths of ribbons, material and colourful stuff, which delineated where she did her performance.
>
> (Holden 2017)

However, for some children, the very fact that feelings *are* so all-consuming means that they may only feel containment *because* of the concrete walls of the playroom (see chapter 5). The challenge for us as therapists is to connect with the child's inner world through the level of attunement we have developed and to be sufficiently self-aware through reflection on what can be called 'parallel processing', the feeling of the feelings which the child is experiencing.

In non-directive play therapy texts, it is difficult to find explicit reference to the notion of transference and countertransference but McMahon (1992:54) comments on the strong feelings that may be unleashed by spontaneous play and how these can leave the therapist feeling overwhelmed. She suggests that if we know about transference, it helps us to *'recognize that the feelings we are experiencing are usually also those of the child towards its parent'*. Our task then as therapist is to 'hold' these strong feelings, to tolerate them, reflect on them and give them back to the child in a more 'manageable' form. This level of containment and attunement allows the child a deeper level of exploration and requires more than the therapist having just a good relationship with the child; it requires an understanding of our own feelings, where they are rooted and how we avoid them intruding into the work with the client, which comes through both personal therapy and the supervision process.

From this chapter, we can see that although play may be difficult to define, it emerges from the transitional space between the infant and the mother figure and allows us to be playful in relationship with our own self, with others and with the environment around us. Play and playfulness enables us to make connections, to process experiences and make sense of our world. Our early care experiences of being held, soothed and attended to promote a sense of having a positive body self that is valued and held in mind by others. We grow to know that we are alive and have substance.

As we grow and develop, the where and how of our play changes. We explore further afield, developing an understanding of how it feels to be 'me', to be an autonomous being. If our early developmental experiences have been negative or abusive, our sense of body self can be non-existent or become distorted and we are likely to experience difficulties with emotional regulation, impulse control and attention and concentration. In order to process these deeply embodied fears and anxieties, we need to be physically active and interactive so that we create new embodied life metaphors which enable us to make and sustain mutually satisfying and fulfilling relationships – with our self, with others in our lives and with the environments we interact with.

References

Aiyegbusi, A. (2004) Touch and the impact of trauma in therapeutic relationships with adults. In White, K. (ed) *Touch, Attachment and the Body*. London: Karnac, pp. 49–56

Bloom, K. (2006) *The Embodied Self: Movement and Psychoanalysis*. London: Karnac

Bowlby, J. (1988) *The Secure Base: Clinical Applications of Attachment Theory*. London: Routledge

Brown, F. and Patte, M. (2013) *Rethinking Children's Play*. London: Bloomsbury

Cell Press (2016) That new baby isn't imitating you. Available from: www.sciencedaily.com/releases/2016/05/160505133848.htm [Accessed 2nd October 2016]

Chown, M. (1963) *Essays on Play*. Unpublished

Chown, A. (2014) *Play Therapy in the Outdoors: Taking Play Therapy out of the Playroom and into Natural Environments*. London: Jessica Kingsley Publishers

Chown, A. (2015) Branching out – developing play therapy in outdoor spaces: A pathway into the unknown. *British Journal of Play Therapy* 11 (Winter), 48–60

Garner, B. P. and Bergen, D. (2006) Play development from birth to age four. In Fromberg, D. P. and Bergen, D. (eds) *Play from Birth to Twelve: Contexts, Perspectives and Meanings* (2nd edition). London: Routledge, pp. 3–12

Glasgow Koste, V. (1995) *Dramatic Play in Childhood: Rehearsal for Life*. Portsmouth: Heinemann

Holden, S. (2017) Email sent to Alison Chown. 6th January

Jennings, S. (1999) *Introduction to Developmental Play Therapy*. London: Jessica Kingsley Publishers

Jennings, S. (2011) *Healthy Attachments and Neuro-Dramatic-Play*. London: Jessica Kingsley Publishers

Learning and Teaching Scotland (2010) *Pre-Birth to Three – Positive Outcomes for Scotland's Children and Families: National Guidance*. Available from: https://education.gov.scot/improvement/Documents/ELC/ELC2_PreBirthToThree/ELC2_PreBirthToThreeBooklet.pdf [Accessed 5th October 2016]

Lester, S. and Russell, W. (2008) *Play for a Change. Play, Policy and Practice: A Review of Contemporary Perspectives*. London: Play England.

McMahon, L. (1992) *The Handbook of Play Therapy*. London: Routledge

Music, G. (2011) *Nurturing Natures: Attachment and Children's Emotional, Sociocultural and Brain Development*. Hove: Psychology Press

Ogden, P., Minton, K. and Pain, C. (2006) *Trauma and the Body: A Sensorimotor Approach to Psychotherapy*. London: W. Norton and Company

Playwork Principles Scrutiny Group (2015) *Statement by the Playwork Principles Scrutiny Group: Playwork Principles*. Available from: www.playboard.org/wp-content/uploads/2015/10/Statement-by-the-Playwork-Principles-Scrutiny-Group-FINAL051015.pdf [Accessed 12th January 2017]

Rizzolatti, G. (2005) The mirror neuron system and imitation. In Hurley, S. and Chater, N. (eds) *Perspectives on Imitation and Imitation in Animals: From Neuroscience to Social Science*. Massachusetts: The MIT Press, pp. 55–76. Available from: https://books.google.co.uk/books?hl=en&lr=&id=qiW3Yc9b6GAC&oi=fnd&pg=PA55&dq=RIzzolatti+monkey+mirror+neurons&ots=n09Skg2GAM&sig=zLMh3J31 6rhv8pCj72kubNdGZRM#v=onepage&q=RIzzolatti%20monkey%20mirror%20 neurons&f=false [Accessed 8th October 2016]

Robertson, J. (2016) *Serious play . . . really!? Explain yourself please!* Lecture given to the BAPT conference, Birmingham, June

Siegal, D. (2011) *Being Versus Doing With Your Child.* [Lecture] Dalai Lama Center for Peace, 11th September. Available from: www.youtube.com/watch?v=PGUEDtGSwW4 [Accessed 24th September 2016]

Sutton-Smith, B. (1997) *The Ambiguity of Play*. London: Harvard University Press.

Totton, N. (2003) *Body Psychotherapy: An Introduction*. Berkshire: Open University Press

Trevarthan, C. (2004) Intimate contact from birth. In White, K. (ed) *Touch, Attachment and the Body*. London: Karnac, pp. 1–16

Van der Kolk, B. (2006) Foreword. In Ogden, P., Minton, K. and Pain, C. (eds) *Trauma and the Body: A Sensorimotor Approach to Psychotherapy*. London: W. Norton and Company, pp. xvii–xxvi

Van der Kolk, B. (2015) *The Body Keeps the Score: Mind, Brain and Body in the Transformation of Trauma*. UK: Penguin Books

Winnicott, D. (1971) *Playing and Reality*. Hove: Brunner–Routledge

Zeedyk, S. (director) (2011) *The Connected Baby* [DVD]. Edinburgh: Jonathan Robertson

Chapter 3

Play in a broader context

There is a broad-based assumption that somehow, in recent decades, the nature of children's play has changed quite radically and perhaps one of the most significant of these changes is the degree to which adults' roles in children's play and leisure activities have increased. On the one hand we have children, often in isolation, looking at screens (TV, tablets, phones) for what can seem a disproportionate amount of their time and on the other, the over-involvement and over-direction of adults through the commercialization of play spaces and activities such as before and after school clubs, soft play areas, holiday play and activity schemes and structured leisure lessons. Perhaps this reflects the need for adults to gain control 'locally' at a time in our society when there is an increasing sense of disempowerment, largely as a result of almost a decade of austerity for the majority of citizens in the face of increasing wealth for an already wealthy minority. Coupled with this, there has been a raft of policies which have seen the gradual erosion of free, state-funded education, health and social care provision, often for the most needy and vulnerable groups in society. That this has been evident to the users of these services but denied by those in office, results in a sense of differing realities and a challenge on our perceptions of what is real which can leave us unsure of ourselves and not just a little confused. Added to this, there is also the impact of increased commercialization which has children and young people as one of its 'target groups', resulting in exploitation by another name. Demands on parents for material possessions as a result of advertising and peer pressure, further fuels the need for parents to feel they have some kind of control over their children. Thomas highlights this, noting:

> a baby of one, a child of six or a young person of 14 … are a product not just of biology and their own immediate environment, but also of the attitudes, habits and expectations built into the culture, the law and the politics of the society in which they are doing their work of 'growing up'.
> (Thomas 2009:8)

Ball et al. (2013:8) comment further on this, recognizing how children's lives are now far more restricted and controlled, and suggest this arises from three similar key factors: cultural, social and economic. As a result of these, they note that: 'children's opportunities to play and explore their neighbourhoods on their own have decreased noticeably, and they spend more time under adult supervision at home, at school and in out-of-school services and activities'. Whilst it is beyond the scope of this book to give full consideration to those policies which have impacted on play and play space, it is important to recognize that the where and how of play is all too frequently determined by adults who are either perceived to be in control, to be an 'expert' or to be working in the best interest of children but with little or no real consultation with them.

Action for Children recently published a downloadable pack for parents entitled 'National Children's Hour – When the Big Hand Reaches for the Little Hand' (2014). It details a range of activities which parents might undertake with their children in order, primarily it would seem, to get them away from the ubiquitous screens that it suggests many of them are anchored to in today's technological climate. Their research showed that this is the single biggest battleground for parents, ahead of the more traditional one of completing homework. Whilst this clearly highlights the pull of screens of all sizes, it does perhaps also beg the question: How have we got to this position where for many young people, reality for a significant portion of their time is virtual? The same research report noted that the activity children would most like to do if they could reclaim an hour of their screen time was to build a den. So why are they not doing this? How have we come to a place where what children want to do – to go outside – and what parents feel is where they should be is precisely where they aren't!

One of the key things that reduces the likelihood of children spending time outdoors is the perceived risk that it poses, primarily from increased traffic but also from 'stranger danger'. In 2013, Play England commissioned a survey for Playday 2013 which found that only some 23% of children played outside at least seven times a week although 40% said they wanted to play out more often. Sadly, only 4% of the children surveyed said they played out in fields and woodlands. It would appear that children's worlds have closed down considerably from the days, not that many decades ago, when many of us were free to roam away from our houses and into a wider environment that encompassed parks and open spaces, fields, woods, streams and beaches. When children were asked what would be needed in order for them to play outside more often, they cited the following:

- less danger from traffic and fewer parked cars
- more time to play
- more of their friends living near them
- more areas to play
- parents and carers giving them more permission to do so
- having more adult supervision available

(Playday 2013)

The issue of danger from traffic and parked cars and the loss of areas for play arises primarily out of continued population growth; the urbanization of our communities and the commensurate increase in car use. The United Nations Department for Economic and Social Affairs reports in the 2014 revision of World Urbanization Prospects that whilst globally the urban population has risen from 30% in 1950 to 54%, within Europe the figure is 75% and in the UK it is around 80% (UN 2014) and for Northern America the figure stands at 82%. The projection for 2050 is a worldwide figure of 66% underlining the rapid growth within urban areas with the associated loss of green space and, hence, much of children's play space. Alongside this, adult concerns about the safety of play and existing play spaces further undermines and marginalizes the more traditional concept of play, despite it being recognized as a human right within the UN Convention on the Rights of the Child (UNCRC).

Well planned and well managed urban green spaces are recognized as being of social, environmental and economic importance with benefits including increased house prices where dwellings are near public green space, increased footfall in green retail spaces and improved physical and mental health. Where there is better management of public spaces and improvement to physical aspects such as increased lighting, there can also be a reduction in crime. Another important aspect of well managed green urban space is that it provides more opportunities for children to engage in creative play; play where they are using their imagination to explore and determine for themselves what shape their play will take (CABE Space, no date).

The idea of children being able to access unrestricted play opportunities underpins the philosophy of the adventure playground movement which began in the UK as early as 1939 with the establishment of a playground in Bolton, Lancashire which contained unusual wooden structures instead of the usual swings, slides and roundabouts. The movement was in part a response to increasing urbanization and an attempt to redress the loss of traditional play spaces. At the same time, there was a shift in philosophy with the recognition of the need for children to be able to play in dedicated playgrounds but where the emphasis was on child focused play, led by the children themselves and not shaped by adult expectations and interpretations of what appropriate play might be. This had arisen as a result of observations of children at play on bombsites both during and after WWII which emphasized the creative nature of children's free, unrestricted play and led to attempts to replicate the opportunities through the establishment of 'junk playgrounds'.

The first of these was a 'reclaimed' bombsite in Camberwell, London. The main advocate of this new type of playground was Marjorie Allen, landscape architect, child welfare campaigner and Baroness of Hurtwood. She had been inspired by her visit to Emdrup, Denmark where she had seen the junk playground established by Carl Theodor Sorenson. He too was a landscape architect and had noticed that the children were not playing in the playgrounds he had designed, but were happier with the debris of the bombsites, construction sites and junkyards. He saw the creative nature of the free play which children engaged in whilst playing in these environments and, as a result, set about creating an enclosed space where children could play in ways that would otherwise be prohibited in traditional playgrounds. This involved the provision of waste materials such as old timber, tyres and netting to furnish them. In addition to the unrestricted nature of this 'junk playground', another key aspect of such play spaces which Allen emphasized was that they fostered a sense of democracy. The local community would be involved in developing the playgrounds out of the bombsites and the children would be the ones who led the play and decided on how the space would be developed (Koslovsky 2007).

Inclusive play

It was out of the adventure playground movement that the idea of integrated play opportunities arose, to ensure there was provision for all developmental and impairment needs – what we might today call inclusive play. An impairment should not become a disability as a result of societal attitudes and values and *all* children need to experience free play. However, John and Wheway (2004) note that it is not accessibility that stops disabled children from 'playing out', rather it is fear and isolation arising as a result of institutional and

Fig 3:1 Inclusive play can happen here

societal discrimination. They suggest that since not all children who are disabled have impaired mobility, inclusive play is not just about accessibility to play equipment, rather it is enabling disabled children to play freely with their friends. The question that needs to be asked, they remind us, is not 'was the playground accessible?', but 'was the disabled child able to play in the playground?' When all children are able to play together, this enriches the experience for everyone and benefits the whole community. This requires us to have a much broader appreciation of what play is and to understand that what adults might view as not playing, for the child concerned is their own play; that is, it is different from our perception of what play should look like. Only by engaging our own playfulness, as we do in the play therapy relationship, and sensitively playing 'in the manner' of a particular child, might we begin to experience their play as it is played. This is not done in order to carelessly mimic, but to enable all children to lead the play, however restricted that play might be.

Although adventure playgrounds were staffed by an adult, they were there to facilitate the play, not dominate it, despite their then title of Play Leader, later changed to Play Worker in recognition of the fact that it is children who lead the play, not the adult worker. Wilson suggests that rather than describe what a playworker is, it is more useful to describe the work they do:

> We look at what is around for the children we seek to serve and for what they are missing. Then we establish an environment that helps compensate for what is missing. Then we watch how children are using the space and share our reflections as a team. Together we make adjustments informed by those observations and reflections. Then we watch some more … *we plan for possibilities*.
>
> (American Journal of Play 2009:269–270, original emphasis)

Because adventure playgrounds were outdoors, simple wooden constructions were created to give some basic shelter from the elements and provide a more intimate gathering space, often with a fire at its centre. There were no facilities and local residents were generally approached for the use of toilets. Many playworkers also kept small animals such as rabbits, guinea pigs, gerbils and even goats and sheep and the children would be fully involved in the care of these. In time, in response to the need to extend the opportunities for play across all seasons, indoor provision was made for a wider range of art and craft-based activities and also for community use for groups such as parents and toddlers. Chilton (2013) notes that despite this, children were still fully involved in the decision to open the space up to such activities, further underlining the democratic ethos which underpins playwork.

Chilton goes on to tell us that in the 1970s there were around 500 adventure playgrounds in the UK but by the late 80s they were in decline as a result of changing social attitudes and increasing consumerism. His thoughts at the time are not only very poignant but also pertinent to the difficulties we face today:

> The country was becoming a society obsessed with consumerism, and social attitudes began to change, shifting gradually but perceptibly, from a nation where street and community life was based on cooperation, the sharing of resources and values and strong neighbourhood support mechanisms, perhaps to one of competition, individualism, prejudice, insularity, territorialism and social independence.
>
> (2013:12)

Shifting attitudes

Chilton believes the death knell for adventure playgrounds sounded as a result of the Health and Safety at Work Act 1974. It was, he feels, not the act itself but the way it was misinterpreted and misapplied resulting in the closure of many playgrounds. Further damage was done by the Children Act of 1989, which determined ratios of adults to children for activities, and set restrictions on the numbers of children able to enter the playgrounds, again as a result of misinterpretation. The Out of School Child Care Initiative diverted money away from playground provision to after school clubs and activities, which rather ironically were generally supported in principle by playworkers, although viewed as more about provision of a workforce than about children's play needs. So here is a clear example of how policies or policy changes, designed to improve things in one area of life, can have the opposite effect and negatively influence other areas such as the how and where of play. The creation of breakfast and after school clubs shifted the 'where' of play for a number of children to schools and the 'how' towards increased adult direction. The responsibility for the organization of such clubs was not always with a trained and qualified playworker either and so access to an adult who understood the nature of children's play and how to facilitate free, creative and self-chosen activity was lost. This seems particularly ironic in light of the survey discussed earlier in which one of the things children say they need in order to feel able to play outside more often is an adult to help them!

As Chilton has suggested, increased consumerism and individualism also played a part in the demise of adventure playgrounds. Changes to social attitudes meant that both the way they operated and how they looked did not sit comfortably alongside what he calls the 'sophisticated designer playgrounds' which began to be marketed. Much of the equipment which was sold commercially was based on structures once created in adventure playgrounds from recycled materials such as net scrambles, wooden forts and low-level linked equipment incorporating planks and tyres. Although many of the playgrounds used today by children contain this type of equipment, there is little or no room for adaption or change as there are rarely any additional materials or junk on hand for children's imagination and creativity to utilize. The other major change to adventure playgrounds is the lack of a professional play-worker. Instead, children must rely on their parents or other accompanying adults. For many this will still provide them with someone who can encourage their experimentation, support them to take a risk and affirm their efforts without being overtly directive. But for some, this will mean they are either left alone to 'get on with it', badgered, cajoled or humiliated into doing it the way the adult thinks it should be done or stopped from playing at anything considered to be too risky.

It was their role as facilitators of creative and unrestricted play that meant playworkers were an important part of children's lives, forging long-lasting, trusting and unique relationships with children and young people who saw in them a non-judgemental adult in whom they might confide. There are, there-fore, strong parallels with play therapy in both the relationship between the playworker and child and the nature of the play they facilitated – experimen-tal, imaginative, exploratory and above all self-determined, an aspect of chil-dren's play that can appear to have been neglected.

Playing out

In the 2013 Playday survey mentioned earlier, children stated that in order to go outside more often, they would need more permission from parents and carers and look for adult supervision once they were outside. The idea of par-ental permission is an interesting one which further emphasizes an increase in adult control of play and play spaces. When I was growing up in the early 1960s, we did ask our parents if we could go out to play or go and call for 'so and so' but also, just as often, our parents would be sending us out to play. This was not a neglectful act, but unless the weather was particularly inclem-ent, outside was where you played with an occasional afternoon indoors to play with games or toys. We lived in a council house with a large garden in an estate on the edge of a town in Wiltshire and there was plenty of additional space to occupy. There was a small green in front of a crescent of houses just up the road, a playing field further away with a large open grassed area for games, and the usual iron structures common at the time, and then there were acres of fields nearby over which we roamed. This is echoed by findings from the adults surveyed for Playday with around 60% of them feeling they had freedom to explore the area around their homes compared with 17% of children today. When we did venture a long way from home, we did so in groups with a span of ages between five and fifteen and we didn't have mobile phones. We had to rely on our own resources, both individual and collective, to problem solve and deal with any crisis that arose. We learned how to co-operate, resolve disputes, negotiate obstacles and generally get along together, and crucially, we learned how to calculate and manage risk.

There was an area of horse chestnut trees on land owned by a particularly fierce farmer, close to the road and beside the railway track. We knew we were tempting fate to go there but that was where the best conkers were to be found and anyway, we had posted the youngest as lookouts! One day when we were happily gathering fallen conkers, we were chased off the land by the very angry farmer waving a shotgun and accompanied by a large Alsatian dog. Fortunately our lookouts were alert to danger and we were speedy, pelting up the bank onto the road before he could get too close. In telling this tale I am advocating neither trespass nor rank stupidity but illustrating how learning can occur when children are left to their own devices, especially in cross-age groups where younger children look to the perceived wisdom of the older ones who in turn develop some idea of group responsibility rather than placing the pursuit of personal goals as of primary importance.

Our consideration of any potential risk was that the farmer rarely came that far, we had posted lookouts and we were close enough to the road to escape and run homeward. This might seem like a somewhat naïve assessment in today's risk-averse society, but incidents like this added to our understanding of danger and dangerous situations, built our resilience and fostered a great spirit of camaraderie in adversity!

From today's climate of heightened anxiety and fear, it is easy to look back and think that everything was golden then. That was not the case, there were accidents, and minor injuries, scrapes and breaks and cuts and bruises, but we pretty much came through without major incident. Our parents knew roughly where we would be and warned us where not to be, not that we always took notice! What was different, however, is that although our parents might have been familiar with the concept of paedophiles and stranger danger, it was not an explicit part of *our* thinking. We had a concept of being careful around one or two known locals but were not aware of the specific concerns, at least not until we were older. In addition to this, we generally played out in a 'gang' where there was safety in numbers. Perhaps now the balance has swung too far the other way and there seems to be a view now that we have to make even very young children aware of every potential danger, not just from traffic but from sexual predators, marginalized groups in society, the internet and from other children. This could be seen as shifting the responsibility for our children's safety away from adults and giving it to the children themselves. Interviewed in the *Guardian* newspaper earlier this year Simon Bailey, chief constable of Norfolk and the National Police Chiefs' Council lead for child protection, suggests that whilst there may not have been an increase in the number of adults with a sexual interest in children, opportunities for them have increased as a result of advancements in technology (Smith 2016). This again highlights a tension in that the increased risk seen as coming from sexual predators in part arises out of the increase in the use of technology which is advertised and marketed in ways aimed to appeal to young people and even young children. To blame paedophilia on corporate greed would be nonsense, but in an economy where profit would appear to be of over-riding importance the balance between protection of our children and the creation of their vulnerability appears to have gone somewhat off course. Getting the balance right between protecting children from harm and increasing their vulnerability is undoubtedly a tricky thing but the more we emphasize the wider vulnerability, the more vulnerable we perceive ourselves to be and therefore the more vulnerable we become. So there is a challenge for us all to ensure that children are allowed to have a childhood devoid of consumerism, commercial exploitation, the effects of poverty and the perceived terrors of modern society, yet one in which they are safe but still have freedom of movement to play and socialize.

Play as a political football...

In 1997, the New Labour Government made a commitment to reduce child poverty and improve the wider life chances, health and education of our children, a move which Stewart (2013) suggests reflected a much more serious focus on early childhood than any previous government. Their key policies centred around three main areas – the introduction of Sure Start Local Programmes and Children's Centres, free early education for three and four year olds and more affordable and better quality childcare, all aimed at reducing inequality and poverty and encouraging parents back to work as a means to this end. Whilst this was laudable in terms of the stated key aim of greater equality, we need to be clear that such policies, designed to encourage people into the workplace to earn as a means to decreasing poverty (and the 'Benefits bill'), also serve the political, commercial and business interests of the country by ensuring a plentiful workforce. This in turn can act to suppress wages for the many, and thereby increase profits for the few, a result which is somewhat at odds with the aims of the original policies.

However, there is clear evidence that investment in early childhood support has long-lasting benefits with some of these not apparent until later in the lives of the children concerned. Between 1997/8 and 2009/10, spending on early years education, childcare and the Sure Start programmes quadrupled. The desire for available and affordable high quality childcare in every neighbourhood was a cornerstone of the Sure Start programme which focused on the five key areas of outreach and home visiting, support for parenting, healthcare and advice, support for parents and children with special educational needs (SEN) and play and learning opportunities (Stewart 2013). The latter of these was underpinned by the concept of the Early Years Foundation Stage (EYFS) as outlined in the Childcare Act 2006. In 2008, to support this, the EYFS curriculum was introduced with the aim of giving all children the best start possible across a number of educational, welfare and developmental domains, including personal, social and emotional (Department for Children, Schools and Families 2008). The identified learning goals were to be met through playful activities and games, including outdoor play with settings providing free-flow play opportunities where children were able to move freely between indoor and outdoor spaces. Garrick et al. (2010), reporting children's own experiences of the EYFS activities, note that where there was access to a fairly large open space and different resources which could be used flexibly, this allowed for more complex and creative play and that most of the children enjoyed physical outdoor activity such as jumping, climbing, chasing, swinging and balancing. However, despite promoting both indoor and outdoor free play, there remained a tension between the idea of free play and activities designed to promote specific outcomes, as Greishaber and McArdle note:

> The way in which play is conceptualised challenges traditional notions of 'free play' and produces concerns about whether play can and should be used to achieve specific educational purposes … It is a difficult debate to have at a time when it appears that we are losing the battle for play in early childhood settings, as regimes of standardised testing, outcomes and academic pushdown overrun the long-established practices of play-based learning.
>
> (2010:90)

So in addition to the commercialization of play, we can also see how in subsequent years, the 'where and how' of play was also affected by demands to meet specified outcomes in early years settings. This did not mean that it was impossible to set up activities where there was a strong element of choice for children, but that play activities were often 'set up' in itself suggests they were not of the children's own making. Where there were unstructured free play opportunities, these still needed to be used to assess the developmental progress of the children and as such it is hard to see how they can be entirely free of adult influence.

It is this adult influence, what might be called 'adultization' of play that has increased almost exponentially. From the freedom to explore ones' own ideas and creativity in an adventure playground, we have moved to the notion of play-based learning where activities are structured to meet learning goals and outcomes, to expensive commercial play spaces, and to, for me, perhaps one of the more curious recent developments – the play date. Children (and parents) have always made arrangements to play or to go to one another's houses and the term date is an adult concept more applicable to a romantic encounter or a business meeting. In relation to play, it suggests a significant degree of adult direction and structure and is also another example of commodification – the idea that everything has to be labelled and made into something rather than remaining the organic process it is.

Whilst the use of play to monitor learning and development might appear a less helpful aspect of the Labour Government's commitment to under-fives, it was under their watch that the first national play strategy was drawn up. This ten year plan, known as the Fair Play Strategy, and funded by the then Department for Children, Schools and Families (DCSF), was to include 3,500 new or refurbished play spaces, with twenty public play spaces plus one adventure playground in each of thirty pathfinder local authorities. A further funding allocation of £1.5 million would see existing third sector adventure playgrounds refurbished. The plan also included a commitment to train 4,000 playworkers to NVQ level 3 and provide continuing professional development to their leaders and managers. Children's centres and schools would offer good quality play provision with Sure Start centres delivering good practice in play and providing information about local play provision. Significant investment was to be made through the 'Building Schools for the Future' (BSF) programme, with clear requirements for schools to provide quality play spaces and for play to be integrated into the OFSTED inspection framework. The strategy was supported by Play England and promised a renewed focus on outdoor opportunities for play.

...kicked out of touch

Sadly, the plan was scrapped by the incoming Coalition Government in 2010 along with the BSF programme. This was despite recognition by the then Deputy Prime Minister, Nick Clegg, that children needed: 'Spaces where they can play, where they can feel completely free, where they can safely push at the boundaries, learning and experimenting. Places where different generations can meet, binding the community together' (Clegg 2010).

Neither the Conservative nor Liberal Democrat manifestos focused specifically on early childhood nor did play feature except as an aspect of early years childcare provision and education. The key policy focus appeared to be on reducing child poverty and greater social mobility. In 2010, a range of independent reviews and reports were commissioned from Field (2010), Poverty and Life Chances; Allen (2011), Early Intervention; Tickell (2011), the EYFS review; Munro (2011), Child Protection; and Nutbrown (2012), Early Education and Childcare Qualifications. Field, Allen, Tickell and Munro were all agreed on the importance of early intervention. This suggested the need for a strong focus on and commitment to the importance of provision of services within the early years and, indeed, the rhetoric of the Coalition Government was that services rather than cash benefits were important. However, the emphasis on services rang rather hollow since this was also a government committed to an economic policy of austerity which in fact saw massive cuts to public services budgets resulting in a reduction in service provision across all sectors.

In addition to this, rather than a focus on the broader agenda of holistic child development, the focus shifted towards educational attainment as evidenced by the renaming of the Department for Children, Schools and Families, to the more traditional Department for Education. This also extended to consideration of children's play where the focus appears to be on improving their sporting prowess and making them healthier, rather than recognizing it as a fundamental right under the UNCRC. Rather than joined up services, overseen by one governmental department, children's and young people's welfare would be overseen by several, flying in the face of international trends towards more integrated services based on sound research evidence.

When the Conservative Government was elected in 2015, despite David Cameron's assurance in the introduction to the party's manifesto (Conservatives 2015) that it was a plan for a better future for families, it did not appear to commit specifically to early intervention to support children's wider development beyond increasing free childcare places for three and four year olds, and two year olds in disadvantaged households, and increasing the number of places in their flagship 'free schools'. Other policy areas were largely related to the economy, infrastructure, changes to the taxation system and welfare reforms. Any consideration of the importance of children's play largely related to the need to get children outside for health reasons; to reduce obesity rates and to get them away from screens. So play, something that comes naturally to children as an activity for leisure for free, has become highly commercialized and a tool of government, used to create learning opportunities which will evidence constructed learning goals and to counter unhealthy lifestyles in part brought about by the commercialization of childhood. As local authorities struggle to prioritize spending as a result of continuous reduction in public funding, provision of high quality play spaces is likely to be under further threat, with advocacy for it now in the hands of the third sector, voluntary and charitable organizations who campaign for high quality provision and, more fundamentally, children's right to play.

The importance of 'risky' play

Incorporated in the concept of children's right to play is access to good quality play spaces which encourage creative play rather than playgrounds where there is an unimaginative and formulaic layout and an overemphasis on safety. The CABE Space document 'Design and Planning for Play' notes that:

> play does not just take place in designated play spaces, but in the whole environment that a child occupies. Future city planning needs to recognise that providing a fenced-off play space in the middle of a housing estate is not adequate – the whole estate should be playable.
>
> (2008:3)

In the case study of the 'eco-district' of Vauban in Germany, they describe how the neighbourhood is virtually car- and road-free with the space instead being given over to children's play. The play here does not happen in defined play spaces but goes on everywhere, much as it did here in the UK decades ago. There are things of interest such as climbing rocks and a sandpit, but the children are free to play where and how they want to without adult interference. The boundaries between garden/street/park and play area have been removed but play is safe because of the absence of traffic. This allows for what we have come to know as 'risky play' but which in reality is play which has not been made artificially safe by being confined to the kind of uninteresting play spaces described earlier.

The Play Safety Forum, an independent body hosted by Play England and formed in 1993, exists to consider and promote the well-being of children and young people through ensuring a balance between safety, risk and challenge in respect of play and leisure provision. In their document 'Managing Risk in Play Provision: Implementation Guide' (Ball et al. 2013), Robin Sutcliffe, Chair of the Forum, writing in the foreword, emphasizes that since children need challenging and exciting places to play this inevitably means managing situations that are inherently risky.

However, parents' fears appear to be not so much connected with injury as a result of play in risky situations, but, as the Playday survey showed, are based around the greater prevalence of traffic today coupled with fear of strangers and a lack of community spirit. In a survey carried out by Eureka Children's Museum of West Yorkshire (Caswell and Warman 2014) only 37% of parents said they let their children go to the end of their street although 95% agreed it was good for children to take risks when playing. Of the parents or carers questioned, 25% said they would not however let their children take these risks without a safe environment to play in even though 81% of children said they preferred playing outside to watching television. It is interesting to note that in relation to risk assessment for school-based activities or educational visits, the law has the concept of the 'prudent parent' in that teachers and anyone in charge of young people have a duty to take such care of their pupils or young people as a prudent parent would (Department for Education (DfE) 2014). Judging from the survey results, this does not leave a lot of room for manoeuvre but does suggest that parents may be being a little overcautious.

So how might we define prudent in relation to the concept of risk in play? The DfE (2014) in its publication for local authorities and education personnel note that a common sense approach should be used in assessing and managing the risks of any activity and that health and safety measures should *help* children experience a wide range of activities, not stop them from engaging in them at all. Perhaps then, a prudent parent is one who recognizes the benefits of children engaging in more risky play and activities and understands the need to minimize such risks, guide them in how to do activities safely and enable them to risk assess for themselves. *'Children and young people need to encounter some real risks if they are to respond positively to challenging situations and learn how to deal with uncertainty. This cannot be achieved by limiting them to supposedly safe environments'* (Wolmuth cited in Ball et al. 2013:99). Without allowing for the development of risk assessment skills in our children and young people, we are placing them in greater danger. Indeed it could be suggested that as adults, our current generation of young people may well be at more serious risk not only in their leisure activities, but also in other day to day activities and in the workplace as a result of being unable to calculate potential risk for themselves and take appropriate action to minimize it.

The field of playwork recognizes that there is need for a balance between risk and the developmental benefits of it to the well-being of children, so that they are protected from harm but have the freedom to develop independence and understand about risk and how to manage it. In this way, learning and development are not stifled by overprotection and adult direction. If we never experience the pleasure of risking ourselves physically how will we know the exhilaration and increase in confidence that comes when we challenge ourselves to cross the borderline between safe and unsafe, to feel fear and conquer it and in so doing, develop a deeper relationship with our body self and know we are alive with possibility?

References

Action for Children (2014) *National Children's Hour – When the Big Hand Reaches for the Little Hand.* Available from: www.actionforchildren.org.uk/media/3607/nch-activity-pack.pdf [Accessed 15th November 2016]

Allen, G. (2011) *Early Intervention: The Next Steps.* Available from: www.gov.uk/government/uploads/system/uploads/attachment_data/file/284086/early-intervention-next-steps2.pdf [Accessed 3rd January 2017]

American Journal of Play (2009) The cultural origins and play philosophy of playworkers: An interview with Penny Wilson. *American Journal of Play* Winter, 269–282. Available from: www.scribd.com/document/119265740/The-Cultural-Origins-and-Play-Philosophy-of-Playworkers-An-Interview-with-Penny-Wilson [Accessed 15th December 2016]

Ball, D., Gill, T. and Spiegal, B. (2013) *Managing Risk in Play Provision: Implementation Guide* (2nd edition). London: National Children's Bureau

CABE Space (no date) *The Value of Public Space: How High Quality Parks and Public Spaces Create Economic, Social and Environmental Value.* Available from: www.designcouncil.org.uk/sites/default/files/asset/document/the-value-of-public-space1.pdf [Accessed 20th November 2016]

CABE Space (2008) *Public Space Lessons: Design and Planning for Play.* Available from: www.designcouncil.org.uk/sites/default/files/asset/document/designing-and-planning-for-play.pdf [Accessed 29th January 2016]

Caswell, R. and Warman, T. (2014) *Play for Today: A Report into the Importance and Relevance of Play for Children and Parents in the UK*. Available from: www.eureka.org.uk/wp-content/uploads/2014/10/Play-for-Today.pdf [Accessed 14th November 2016]

Childcare Act (2006) Available from: www.legislation.gov.uk/ukpga/2006/21 [Accessed 20th September 2016]

Chilton, T. (2013) *Adventure Playgrounds: A Brief History*. Available from: www.fair-playforchildren.org/pdf/1397922953.pdf [Accessed 21st October 2016]

Clegg, N. (2010) *Deputy Prime Minister's Speech on Children and Families.* [Presentation] Barnardos, 17th June. Available from: www.gov.uk/government/speeches/deputy-pms-speech-on-children-and-families [Accessed 23rd October 2016]

Conservatives (2015) *Strong Leadership, a Clear Economic Plan, a Brighter More Secure Future*. Available from: www.conservatives.com/manifesto [Accessed 3rd November 2016]

Department for Children, Schools and Families (2008) *Statutory Framework for Early Years Foundation Stage: Setting the Standards for Learning, Development and Care for Children from Birth to Five*. Available from: www.lse.ac.uk/intranet/LSEServices/nursery/pdf/statutoryframework.pdf [Accessed 28th September 2016]

Department for Education (2014) *Health and Safety: Advice on Legal Duties and Powers for Local Authorities, School Leaders, School Staff and Governing Bodies*. Available from: www.gov.uk/government/publications/health-and-safety-advice-for-schools [Accessed 12th January 2017]

Field, F. (2010) *The Foundation Years: Preventing Poor Children from Becoming Poor Adults.* Available from: http://webarchive.nationalarchives.gov.uk/20110120090128/http://povertyreview.independent.gov.uk/media/20254/poverty-report.pdf [Accessed 12th November 2016]

Garrick, R., Bath, C., Dunn, K., Maconochie, H., Willis, B. and Wolstenholme, C. (2010) *Children's Experiences of the Early Years Foundation Stage*. Available from: www.gov.uk/government/uploads/system/uploads/attachment_data/file/182163/DFE-RR071.pdf [Accessed 28th September 2016]

Greishaber, S. and McArdle, F. (2010) *The Trouble With Play*. Berkshire: Open University Press

John, A. and Wheway, R. (2004) *Can Play – Will Play: Disabled Children and Access to Outdoor Playgrounds*. Available from: www.fieldsintrust.org/Upload/Documents/Products/can_play_will_play_1004006374.pdf [Accessed 28th January 2017]

Kozlovsky, R. (2007) Adventure playgrounds and postwar reconstruction. In Gutman, M. and De Coninck-Smith, N. (eds) *Designing Modern Childhoods: History, Space, and the Material Culture of Children; An International Reader*. Available from: www.adventureplay.org.uk/RK%20Adventure%20Playground.pdf [Accessed 21st November 2016]

Munro, E. (2011) *The Munro Review of Child Protection. Final Report, a Child-centred System*. Available from: www.gov.uk/government/uploads/system/uploads/attachment_data/file/175391/Munro-Review.pdf [Accessed 17th December 2016]

Nutbrown, C. (2012) *Foundations for Quality: The Independent Review of Early Education and Childcare Qualifications – Final Report*. Available from: www.gov.uk/government/uploads/system/uploads/attachment_data/file/175463/Nutbrown-Review.pdf [Accessed 18th December 2016]

Playday (2013) *2013 Opinion Poll.* Available from: http://playday.gn.apc.org/2013-opinion-poll/ [Accessed 30th September 2016]

Smith, J. (Thursday 10 March 2016) *Protecting children from paedophiles means sacrificing their innocence.* Available from: www.theguardian.com/commentisfree/2016/mar/10/protecting-children-paedophiles-sacrificing-innocence-sex-relationship-education [Accessed 26th November 2016]

Stewart, K. (2013) *Labour's Record on the Under Fives: Policy, Spending and Outcomes, 1997–2010.* Available from: http://sticerd.lse.ac.uk/dps/case/spcc/wp04.pdf [Accessed 12th October 2016]

Thomas, N. (2009) Children, young people and politics in the UK. In Montgomery, H. and Kellett, M. (eds) *Children and Young People's Worlds: Developing Frameworks for Integrated Practice.* Bristol: Policy Press, pp. 7–22

Tickell, C. (2011) *The Early Years: Foundations for Life, Health and Learning. An Independent Report on the Early Years Foundation Stage for Her Majesty's Government.* Available from: www.gov.uk/government/uploads/system/uploads/attachment_data/file/180919/DFE-00177-2011.pdf [Accessed 15th December 2016]

United Nations (2014) *World Urbanization Prospects – 2014 Revision.* Available from: www.esa.un.org/unpd/wup/Publications/Files/WUP2014-Highlights.pdf [Accessed 4th October 2016]

Chapter 4

Play therapy in nature – meanings and metaphors

At one with ourselves

The author Ian McEwan has said '*The self, like a consumer durable, may be plucked from the shelves of a personal identity supermarket; a ready-to-wear little black number*' (2016).

He made this comment in relation to whether gender is something people can define for themselves, and was heavily criticized for it. But perhaps there is more than a grain of truth in this idea if one looks wider than gender politics to the broader spectrum of the self. Orbach (2009:5) suggests that:

> Late capitalism has catapulted us out of centuries' old bodily practices which were centred on survival, procreation, the provision of shelter and the satisfaction of hunger. Now birthing, illness and ageing, whilst part of the ordinary cycle of life, are events that can be interrupted or altered by personal endeavour in which one harnesses the medical advances and surgical restructuring on offer.

Kumar (2015:24), in considering the link between soil, soul and society, what he describes as a 'new trinity for our time', tells us that if we are to find a more harmonious way of living with the natural world – the soil – then we will need to consider finding a way to create harmony within our soul through self-knowledge. He tells us that this type of self-knowledge allows us to understand that we are but a small part of a greater whole, or what he describes as 'an integral organ of the earth'. This kind of insight into our self is very different from the ego focused sense of self which exists in no small part in today's society. Kumar also reflects that in focusing so narrowly on ideas of religion, race, class, gender and other divisive constructs and concepts, we can become bogged down in a state of 'I', and can become isolated from 'others'. So perhaps what we currently have in social culture is the idea that we can control and change almost everything about us, McEwan's idea of the 'off-the-shelf self'. However, the parameters of such changes are also very narrowly defined by what Orbach (2009:12) describes as the '*homogenous visual culture promoted by industries that depend on the breeding of insecurity*'.

So why is this important? If you watch small children, particularly those under three or four, there is generally a freedom of the body by which I mean a lack of self-consciousness and inhibition. They run and jump, crawl and dance, spin and squat down with apparent effortless ease. And then something changes; they become aware not of themselves but of the self as reflected in others who make judgements, who disapprove, who criticize, who make them feel uncomfortable and shameful. There is a growing body of evidence to suggest that children as young as four and five are developing quite fixed ideas about how their bodies should look and becoming familiar with ways to lose weight. Advertising images play a significant part in this, as do the rather stereotypical images of key characters in children's films and television programmes. The sense of our body self, developed in that earliest contact with our mother figure and other family members, which should leave us with positive feelings can become distorted by the culture in which our families live and which lives in us through our familial contacts. Orbach refers to this as a *dis-ease*.

Dislocation

The pressure to conform to social and cultural ideals appears to have increased quite significantly over recent decades and is a multi-million pound and dollar business selling beauty products designed to keep us looking young, slimming products, natural or health foods designed to keep our bodies in peak condition and conforming to the one acceptable and slender shape, multi-vitamins, minerals and juices to keep visits to the doctor at a minimum and cosmetic procedures to nip, tuck or plump most areas of the body. We are encouraged to remove unsightly blemishes, all body hair, excess fat, wrinkles and spots – in fact anything that marks the path through life our bodies have carried us on.

Those who still take part in manual, physical work have body shapes and contours which reflect what they do. But such is the sedentary nature of much of today's work that we are driven to shape our bodies at the gym, in the fitness studio or out running on the streets and there is a plethora of 'celebrity' fitness programmes we can download onto our phones and into our living rooms. We can believe that the body we have is no longer acceptable unless we have worked it, primped it, preened it, smoothed it, sculpted it and dressed it in the high fashion of whichever group we feel we belong to. To do much of this, however, we need disposable income, thereby putting such activities beyond the means of those on a restricted budget and creating further divisions within society.

The pressure to conform to standardized body images, to be perfectly groomed and turned out is fuelled by high pressure advertising aimed at exploiting our insecurities and thus encouraging us to buy an ever increasing range of products, activities and services. Alongside this there is an increasing push by advertisers towards the benefits of particular lifestyles. In these increasingly consumerist times, many people want to reconnect with nature because they see the harm we are doing to our natural world and how we are consuming resources at an unsustainable rate. Others, however, fall prey to the promotion of the rural idyll – a life in the country and an 'appetite' to be satisfied, as evidenced by the following extract from the website of a new 'community of sustainable holiday homes' to be built in the South West:

> [This] is an exciting new development of sustainable holiday homes created in the wildly beautiful environs of … [and] set among historic heathland, woodland and lakes … [It] provides the ultimate retreat for families craving a slice of the real British outdoors … the vision is to transform an unspoilt nature reserve into a residential community with a strong sense of security yet boundless opportunities to explore the natural world.
>
> (silverlakedorset no date)

The development aims to provide a sustainable solution to a disused quarry, provide some 750 jobs, though not all of these locally, and increase local investment by around £470 million over the next three decades. Not unnaturally, it has therefore been welcomed by both the local residents and Parish Council, for those living in rural areas need employment opportunities and local businesses need investment. There is a paradox, however, for this type of rural community is far away from the reality of living in the country for the many residents who experience lack of basic opportunities such as transport links, employment and affordable housing. That this has happened is in part because the countryside and many of our coastal towns are seen as a bit of a playground for those with plenty of disposable income who can afford a second home, or a place in a gated community. This influx of wealth has pushed up house prices and rents way beyond the means of many whose only homes are in rural communities. There is also a curious contradiction here in the idea of an unspoilt nature reserve being transformed into a gated residential 'holiday' community, when it could have been made publicly accessible to all for leisure and pleasure.

Perhaps it is disconnection and dissatisfaction that drives us to take our constructed off-the-shelf selves and drop them into a lifestyle which says that we live in the country, that we like being outdoors and being in a 'natural' environment. There is a further paradoxical nature to all of this for as much as we want to appear at home and at ease with Mother Nature, we want to structure her to suit our risk-averse, 'make it safe, secure and sanitary' selves. But the outdoors is by its very nature both beautiful and unpredictable. It can be messy, dirty, dangerous and even terrifying – in short it is uncontrollable. This makes for an uneasy bedfellow in today's tightly controlled society where all risk must be finely calculated and taken away before we dare to undertake an activity or put our children in a new environment. Nature should not be seen as a space to be 'owned' by someone but one that is shared by us all and in which we live harmoniously with her and with all other beings who inhabit her.

Working in nature and with nature

Taking play therapy into the outdoors is not about buying into this current agenda of getting back to nature on a superficial level. Nature provides a rich sensory experience vital to our development in general and our body self in particular. If we spend time with her, just as she presents herself, we will see that she offers us a new and much more democratic context for our work where the space belongs to neither of us yet to both of us and through the therapeutic alliance we build with our clients, 'symbolic' walls are created which contain the work safely (see fig 4:1). We need to seize every opportunity to realign our relationship with nature in order to understand that what she offers to us is a place for meditation and transformation, for a peaceful appreciation of our dependence upon her for our survival and a mirror in which are reflected our own intimate relationships. By using outdoor settings as well as the traditional 'playroom', we can create a context for the children we work with to develop an appreciation of a containing relationship with the 'nature mother' that may provide them with a lifelong therapist and lead them to actively engage in her protection,

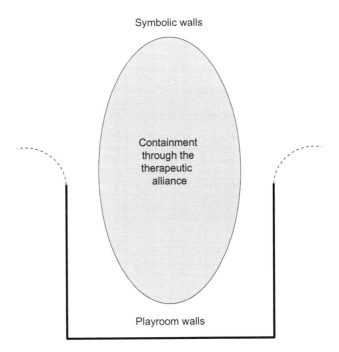

Symbolic walls

Containment through the therapeutic alliance

Playroom walls

Fig 4:1 Symbolic walls of the therapeutic relationship – the container for work in nature

driven by their acknowledgement of her not as separate from them but as embodied within them.

That nature is dynamic and ever changing adds a further dimension to our work. Beth Collier, a nature-based psychotherapist working with adults, who uses London's green spaces as her therapy room, gives articulate voice to this important aspect: '*Nature is always changing, sometimes the therapy room is decorated with sunshine, cloud, rain, birds, people, flowers, leaves or bare branches. It can be light, cold, hot or wet. We never know how she will present herself*' (2016).

Whilst it is this unpredictability that may deter many therapists from using outdoor spaces, it is an aspect of nature which reflects our lives and the unforeseen events which can occur in them. Different landscapes can offer differing metaphorical examples of this as we see in chapter 5. In today's over-controlled, over-marketed and exploitative society, we need to make time to return to the realness of nature, to get away from the constant chatter that bombards us from all sides encouraging us to relate to one another through some electronic means and remember what it feels like to connect through our bodies, our physicality and all of our senses. In this way, we will get to know ourselves better, to really be able to sit with ourselves and find some peace. For our young clients, nature offers a more concrete way of seeing ourselves and our lived life. Much like the resources we have in the playroom, the real and viscerally felt experience and the metaphors which abound offer us a way of seeing and understanding ourselves that does not rely on words.

A relationship with 'place'

For therapists, the relationship we have developed with nature is also under-pinned by our own experiences, personal beliefs and values. I spent my early childhood grubbing in the earth alongside my father while he did the serious job of growing the family's vegetables. My hands have been in the earth ever since as I too love to garden and grow vegetables. Writing this, I am reminded of more words from Satish Kumar: '*Soil is the source of all life, literally and metaphorically. All life comes from the mother soil and returns to her. Soil contains earth, air, fire and water. She is nature herself*' (2015:9). This idea of earth or soil as a mother figure is also present in Aboriginal culture.

> The Aboriginals ... love the earth and all the things of the earth. [We] come to literally love the soil, we sit or recline on the ground with a feeling of being close to a mothering power ... The soil is soothing, strength-ening, cleansing and healing.
>
> (Pattel-Gray 1991 cited in Stockton 1995:86)

In working with the soil, I feel *grounded* which in my mind means connected to nature by the earth and through the earth. In my later childhood, out with friends, our playground was the nearby green and playing field, but also the surrounding farmland where we would wander for hours on end, constructing dens, working out how to cross streams and brooks without getting water in our wellies – not always a successful mission – and, as I see now from the viewpoint of adult reflection, learning how to work together, to collaborate to assess risk and manage adversity. This was our world, we inhabited it; it had meaning for us and we had an attachment to it, strong enough to pull me back there just to stand and view it – to be there again in the years when I was grown-up and lived away from it. I particularly love being by the sea and when my brother traced our family tree, there were many relatives who had worked on and with the sea in one capacity or another as well as several farmers. The outdoors, I believe, is in my blood – it is within me – embodied trans-generationally. I am at home outdoors and I count myself as lucky in this respect. For others, it remains a place of purgatory; a place that is not only unpredictable, harsh and fear provoking, but also home to things that bite and sting, things that can appear from nowhere to unnerve or even to terrify and things which can poison and contaminate.

These points of view may be considered as perhaps two rather polar extremes of a continuum of our attitude towards and our comfort of being in outdoor spaces but how we *feel* in nature is an obvious key component of working outside. When we are out with our clients, we need to be aware of the attachment they have with nature and how this in turn relates to the style of attachments they have with others in their lives.

There are of course other perspectives of nature – from spiritual connectedness to environmental concern, from recognition of its healing power to enjoyment of outdoor activities. What nature represents to us and for us will have an effect on both our psychological and emotional well-being, something that has become far more widely recognized and accepted in recent years. The word *topophilia*, coming from the Greek topos – place, and philia – love of, describes the emotional connectedness with or love of a place or an environment, and typically with a 'natural' place. This idea of our having an emotional bond with the natural environment is at the heart of ecopsychology and the idea that in order to heal the mind, we must restore the earth, reflecting today's perceived widespread disconnection from nature. The notion of a 'sense of place' can also be linked with our cultural identity where culture is understood to mean distinctive learned and shared behaviours, transmitted or expressed by language or conventional symbols (Stockton 1995; Sutton and Anderson 2004) or as Stockton more specifically describes it '*the supportive mothering environment of one's personal development*' (1995:5).

So we might agree that there appears to be a broadly understood concept of place attachment which evolves from the meaning and understanding of a specific place and the emotional connection we have with it. In studying geography, there are two strands: physical geography – the study of the natural environment – and human geography, which considers the relationship between humans and their natural environment which focuses on a sense of place. However, as Morgan (2010) notes, place as a concept has a meaning which is easy to grasp, yet a definition which is elusive. The idea of place attachment or attachment to a place is an interesting one and suggests that it can be a two-way process in that whilst we may have an attachment to a particular place, *it* can offer us some of the qualities of the attachment relationship experienced between the mother figure and the infant and provide a second intermediate playground since we can feel held by it (Chown 2014).

Tuan (1977) suggests that to children, place may represent something of value providing nurture and support. Their understanding of it starts with their mother figure who they see as an object of dependable comfort. As they grow, their attachment extends to include other objects and familiar localities. They may develop ambivalent feelings towards some of these if they are a source of both comfort and concern. An illustration of this is how a child might regard the locality of their cot as both a pleasurable, cosy world but one in which they also feel alone and fearful. The idea of place becomes more nuanced and sophisticated as children become more geographically aware, with small children focusing more on the people within a place rather than the physical features of it. Tuan makes the point that public places are not made to the scale of children and they feel the need to be in places that fit them,

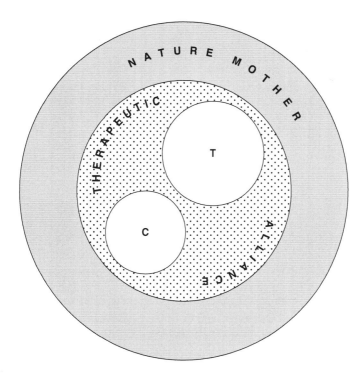

Fig 4:2 The second intermediate playground

'*seek[ing] out nooks and corners both in man-made environments and in nature*' (1977:32). He tells us that although adults' attachment to place may be rooted in the sentiment of history, children live predominantly in the present and the future and live through their imagination and actions. Therefore, places which hold significant meaning to adults may have none for a child.

> The therapist was working on a small rocky beach with four boys. At the rear of the beach there were huge boulders that formed part of the sea defences. Between the boulders were small spaces that led to slightly bigger spaces beneath. Two of the boys spotted a 'crack' between two of the rocks barely big enough for them to crawl through. They wriggled and squeezed their way in, hovering on the borderline between fear – of getting stuck – and the delight of having found their own special place to hide away from others. They managed to both squeeze into the space beyond but had to curl up almost in a foetal position to both be able to sit. How wonderful this must have felt, to be in that womblike space, together. They were only able to stay in there for ten minutes or so before they burst out squealing that their legs and arms were aching from being all folded up! Each time the group visited the beach, the boys returned to their 'cave' and refused to let anyone else in. The therapist wondered what it was like to have such a special space to share. 'It's great, it's ours, just ours!'
>
> She reflected that they must feel very safe in there even though it was cold rock and only a small space. 'As long as the tide don't come in and drown us. Keep watch will you?'

Macfarlane highlights this aspect of children's connection to nature suggesting that for them:

> nature is full of doors – nothing but doors really – they swing open at every step. A hollow in a tree is a gateway to a castle. An ant hole in dry soil leads to the other side of the world … what we bloodlessly call 'place' is to young children a wild compound of dream, spell and substance: place is somewhere they are always *in*, never *on*.
>
> (2015:315)

This could not have been more true of the boys in their rock cave. As adults, because we have had many different experiences, places may come to have meaning for sentimental reasons so they can be both comforting or uncomfortable. For most of us, there will however be some place which has the capacity to calm us and restore equilibrium or homeostasis, the balance within us.

Whilst it may not always be the exact same place that we visit to feel restored, we will experience the same feelings within:

> I paddled west for three hours, straight out to sea. I had travelled six or seven miles from the shore, further than I had been before but I had still not found the place ... every time I go I seek this place, a place in which I feel a kind of peace I have never found on land ... my place was here; a here that was always different but always felt the same; a here that seemed to move further from the shore with every journey.
>
> (Monbiot 2014:16)

Morgan (2010), in discussing the multiple and differing definitions of place attachment, tells us that the humanistic approach recognizes the deeper significance of place in people's lives which comes from the relationship they have and the emotional quality of this. The word 'resonance' might therefore come into play here, the definitions of which include 'character', 'quality', 'tone', 'reverberation' and 'echo'. A place or a landscape can resonate with us, it can transport us back to childhood, stir a memory of a particular event, occasion or person or touch us in some other way that stirs our emotions, reverberates within us and echoes the past so that we experience 'place' in an embodied way – beyond the merely cognitive, in a visceral, internalized manner.

Philip Marsden in his book *Rising Ground: A Search for the Spirit of Place* (2014:23) discusses what he calls the 'scholarly argy-bargy' that surrounds the difference in definitions between 'place' and 'space'. Perhaps here, in this chapter, we do not need scholarly discussions of whether there is clear 'evidence' about the existence of the concept of place attachment or of the idea of a sense of place. Perhaps it is just enough to accept that if we are open to it, we do feel connections to places and environments; we feel 'at home' in them, rested and calmed or at other times tested and unnerved by them. Perhaps all we need to be clear about is that if we are working in natural, outdoor places, we need to be aware of the meaning they hold for us and be attuned to our clients in a way that allows us to be open to any meanings they hold for them. And perhaps there is something about these places that can give us not only a sense of belonging, or of connecting with, but also offer us an understanding of *our* place within a bigger 'landscape', a sense of belongingness to something beyond us that we may not be able to put into words.

References

Chown, A. (2014) *Play Therapy in the Outdoors: Taking Play Therapy out of the Playroom and into Natural Environments.* London: Jessica Kingsley Publishers

Collier, B. (2016) *Nature's therapy room: A day in the life.* [Handout from training day] 23rd September

Kumar, S. (2015) *Soil, Soul, Society: A New Trinity for Our Time*. Sussex: Leaping Hare Press

Macfarlane, R. (2015) *Landmarks*. London: Hamish Hamilton

Marsden, P. (2014) *Rising Ground: A Search for the Spirit of Place*. London: Granta

McEwan, I. (2016) *Examining the Self*. [Lecture] The Royal Institution, 31st March. Available from: www.rigb.org/whats-on/events-2016/march/public-examining-the-self [Accessed 2nd September 2016]

Monbiot, G. (2014) *Feral: Rewilding the Land, Sea and Human Life*. London: Penguin Books

Morgan, P. (2010) Towards a developmental theory of place attachment. *Journal of Environmental Psychology* 30 (1), 11–22

Orbach, S. (2009) *Bodies*. London: Profile Books Limited

silverlakedorset (no date) *The Vision*. Available from: http://silverlakedorset.com/vision/ [Accessed 5th January 2017]

Stockton, E. (1995) *The Aboriginal Gift, Spirituality for a Nation*. Alexandria: Millennium Books

Sutton, M. Q. and Anderson, E. N. (2004) *Introduction to Cultural Ecology*. Oxford: Alta Mira Press

Tuan, Y. (1977) *Space and Place: The Perspective of Experience*. London: University of Minnesota Press

Chapter 5

Getting started – practical, ethical and philosophical considerations

Since there remains very little written specifically about the practice of play therapy in the outdoors, guidance on best practice in outdoor learning and education and psychotherapeutic work with adults have helped to inform this chapter. The areas considered also result from questions I have been asked by therapists, students and those attending my workshops and provide a focus for considering the issues most likely to arise when setting out to move your practice outdoors. It does not seek to provide an instruction manual or a definitive guide, rather it is a reflection of the pathways those who are already working in nature have trodden.

The BAPT Play Therapy Core Competences state that in order to develop and manage a playroom/ play therapy environment, we need to:

> Take responsibility for the development and safe management of the play therapy environment/play room, in line with Health & Safety standards. This includes selection and maintenance of play materials, risk assessment of the environment and taking appropriate steps to ensure continuing safety; ensuring privacy during sessions, preserving confidentiality in use and storage of therapeutic materials produced in sessions.
>
> (BAPT 2014)

When we begin to think about moving from the playroom, there are some basic issues that need consideration such as:

- safeguarding
- insurance
- first aid training

However, what we need to be mindful of is that if we choose to move our practice into nature, the same 'standards' apply as when we are working in the playroom although clearly there are some adaptions which will need to be made to take account of issues such as the privacy of the space and the confidentiality of any therapeutic materials which may be produced which will be discussed further later in the chapter.

In order to practise as play therapists and to maintain any voluntary registration that might apply to us, in addition to any membership of a relevant professional body, we need:

- safeguarding training, generally at least level 2
- our own public liability and professional indemnity insurance (although if you are employed by an organization or agency you may be covered by their insurance)
- basic first aid knowledge, helpful in an emergency and useful in everyday life

In addition to this, we are required both by our professional bodies and the Professional Standards Authority with which we may be registered to maintain a log of our continuing professional development (CPD).

What resources will I need?

As play therapists, when we set up our playroom, we have already made choices about what resources we will have in them, frequently based on the suggestion of our training institutions. Resources which offer the child the opportunities to engage in the full range of embodiment, projection and role activities including natural materials are usual but we are relatively free to choose how we present these so it is always worth reflecting on why we have made these choices in supervision so that we are clear that our choices are relevant to each client. (See appendix 4 for list of additional resources you will need.)

When we move beyond the playroom we will need to agree what, if anything, can be taken out; reflecting on our decision will ensure it is right for the child. Nature outside the playroom provides us with a different but additional set of resources in that not only is there often a wider range of materials that the child can manipulate and use in the sand tray, image making and construction but there is also a rich sensory resource in the sights, sounds and feel of natural surroundings. If, as we discussed in chapter 4, we consider nature as a co-therapist, then there is also the added dimension of both our own and our clients' relationship with her.

Where or how do I start?

During a recent Play Therapy in the Outdoors (PTITO) workshop, this question generated a lot of interesting discussion highlighting both the demands of our training courses and the different settings in which we all work. For those who are training, the guiding principle is that we need to learn to hold the therapeutic frame in a traditional playroom setting before we consider moving into the outdoors. Once we have qualified and are confident to do this, making the move outside depends on two things to which we may give equal weight: our sense of competent therapist self and whether leaving the playroom is right for our client.

How long do I work with a child before moving outside?

> Nothing happens without at least a thread of a relationship. The relationship is a tenuous thing that takes careful nurturing. It is the foundation of the therapeutic process and can, in and of itself, be powerfully therapeutic.
>
> (Oaklander 1988:293)

In determining whether or not a child is ready to move outdoors, my guiding principle would be to 'know' your client and hold their needs as central to your decision making but also know yourself, particularly your sense of competent therapist 'self'; are you ready to step out? It is crucial that you also check in with your supervisor and reflect on the root of any concerns you may have so you are clear about whether they need to be taken to personal therapy or can be resolved through the supervision process. The effective use of supervision is something which is enshrined in all professional organizations' codes of conduct or ethics. Entering into personal therapy is a stipulation of most, although not all, therapeutic trainings and provides us with the opportunity to experience the process we will take our clients through at first hand, so allowing us understanding of our own emotional world and a view of the therapeutic process from both perspectives (Jordan 2015).

Although moving play therapy sessions beyond the playroom door remains part of the overall therapeutic process, it is helpful to see it also as having a unique structure of its own but one which sits very comfortably within that overall therapeutic process. From my work in outdoor settings, I have come to see this structure as three phases (see fig 5:1). The *settling* phase is where we get to know each other and the therapeutic alliance is established; *transition* occurs when the child feels ready and able to step beyond the playroom, and in the final phase, the child is working at a deeply therapeutic level and *transformation* can occur.

I always start my sessions with a child or group of children in the playroom so we can first get to know each other and move towards establishing a therapeutic alliance, the relationship we need to provide the container for our work, wherever that work might be; the idea of symbolic walls. It is at this stage that I would include the idea of incorporating the use of an outdoor space and, if appropriate, offer the child/ren a visit to see it. Although the use of an outdoor space is raised, I do also ensure that there is an understanding that we will spend time getting to know each other in the playroom first so that we will

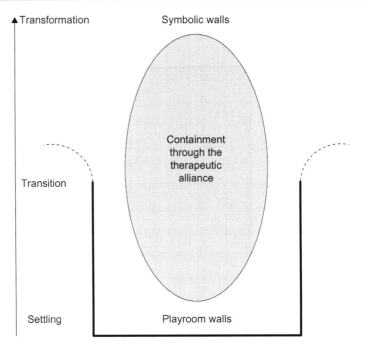

Fig 5:1 The three stages of play therapy in nature – settling, transition and transformation

both know when we are ready to go there. However, for the reasons discussed below, since the therapist holds the responsibility for ensuring the physical and emotional safety of the client, the final word must rest with her.

Towards a more equal relationship

In building a relationship which is mutually satisfying and productive, for this is what the therapeutic relationship is, we need to be aware that we are not adopting the role of a parent, but rather providing a blank canvas for our client to work on. In setting clear boundaries and limits, we remain authentic; our own person, and support children's potential to be the same. In this way we co-construct a democratic relationship which recognizes that each is an integral part of what is happening and each has equal value in this partnership. '*It facilitates an appropriate and healthy emotional bond where the purpose of the therapy is recognised by both but may be explicitly spoken by neither*' (Chown 2014:119). We as the adult in non-directive work come to it without expectations of the child, without the need to steer the process or control the space but are ready to accompany them on their unique metaphorical pathway. When we move outdoors, the pathway becomes real and the sense of democracy is enhanced because the space we are in belongs to neither but to both.

As a general rule, once I feel that there is a strong therapeutic alliance and that to move outside would not prejudice my client's safety, I remind them of the possibility of going outside much as I will sometimes reflect that *'there might be something in the room that you can use to show me how you feel'*. It becomes merely an extension of the existing space and resources. Sometimes, a child will ask almost immediately if they can go outside. Then, as part of limit setting, I gently remind them of our conversation about us needing to get to know each other first before we can agree we are ready but that once we have done that, we can come back to the idea of going outside. I do not see this as causing a tension with the idea of a democratic relationship since limit setting is an important part of the therapeutic process with children.

The guiding principles for the use of limits in non-directive (democratic) therapy are that they should reflect the practical reality of the constraints imposed by the physical context in which the therapy is conducted and should address the needs of the child (Wilson et al. 1992:205).

A joint decision

Generally speaking, because I work in schools, there is an outdoor space literally just beyond the playroom door. If the child is curious, we may visit the place together in our early sessions or the offer may just remain 'in the air' so that the child knows they can venture out and we can make the decision together if and when they are ready. Any concerns I may have had about moving to work in the outdoors relating to a particular individual client will have been taken to supervision. In adult psychotherapy in the outdoors, negotiation with the client is possible in a way that it isn't when we are working with children. Full discussion of the pros and cons of being in either a public or potentially shared space are not really appropriate unless the young person is of an age and stage of development where their ability to take an autonomous decision competently can be assured. This is particularly so since in 'discussions' with most adults, children often feel they must give the right answer – the one they perceive as being sought by the adult. However, this does not preclude some level of negotiation where it is appropriate but we need to be realistic about how much is possible (see appendix 1 – The issue of competency).

As play therapists, we use our professional judgement to decide if and when a child is able to make or contribute towards an informed decision about the location of the sessions. Our professional organizations' codes of conduct and good practice guidance recognize that we may have to make challenging ethical decisions about our work in relation to our client's needs and note that there must always be careful consideration of their capacity to give consent. It may also be that some of the challenges in making these decisions come from the tension between different ethical principles, and discussion in supervision will support your decision making and enable you to uphold these ethical responsibilities. When the child and I decide we are ready to step outside, I have already used my professional judgement to consider whether or not we have a secure therapeutic relationship that will be able to provide a safe container for the work. In supervision, I will also have discussed if leaving the playroom is right for the young person. In this way, we can feel confident that we have kept our client and their needs as central to our decision making, whilst remaining mindful of our responsibilities and duty of care to work in their best interest and not to cause them harm.

Should I expect to work outdoors with every client?

It needs to be clearly noted here that for some children, moving out of the playroom is not appropriate because the feelings they experience can be so overwhelming that they continue to need the security of both the therapeutic alliance, and 'concrete' walls in order to feel contained. They may be struggling with limits and boundaries and find the freedom they experience outdoors too overwhelming and are unable to bring themselves back to some degree of homeostasis at the point at which we need to return indoors to end the session.

The experience of one non-directive play therapist and social worker who is part of a multi-professional Child and Adolescent Mental Health Services (CAMHS) team and who uses an outdoor space illustrates this point:

> I was thinking about a child I am now seeing that I considered taking outdoors, but, because unusually, it took at least twelve sessions for him to develop trust and a relationship with me, and for me to believe it needed to be **me** in the room rather than any adult, I thought, to go outdoors might dilute the intensity of the experience. It therefore somehow felt more appropriate to stick with the containment and intensity the room offers. I thought the outdoors might offer too many distracting opportunities for him to 'avoid' developing the relationship deeper [either] the space was too large or [he might] put himself at a physical distance from me thus avoiding the connection. Suffice to say – I have my last session with him next week, so something's gone right!
>
> (Holden 2017)

For this client, moving into nature would have prejudiced the developing relationship and undermined the therapeutic process. The therapist's consideration of the appropriateness of an outdoor space was a form of risk assessment; taking into account whether the benefit to the client was greater than the risk posed and accepting that in this case it was not. This concept of risk/benefit assessment is helpful in that it provides a focus not only for considering physical risk, but also the broader concept of risk as including emotional or psychological safety.

This is also true of the following case study:

Steven is seven. He is in foster care for the fourth time, each time he has been with a different set of carers. He has three siblings who are all with different carers. He sees two of them regularly but not often, through arranged and supervised contact, but has daily contact with another as they both attend the same school. He suffered neglect in his early years and there are concerns from school staff and his therapist that he may have seen sexually explicit and inappropriate material or have been sexually abused although neither has yet been proven.

During therapy sessions, his play is highly repetitive in its storylines and he always takes on a role where he is the 'baddie' or the robber and has to be chased and imprisoned but escapes continually and so has to be killed. He tells the therapist she must shoot him in the head, between the eyes. When he makes this request, he speaks in a low, aggressive voice, and is insistent that he must die. He finds it very difficult to come out of role. During these stories and particularly when he insists on being killed, the feeling of desolation, isolation and despair are almost palpable. It needs both the therapist and the walls of the room to contain it. The therapist feels that to move outside of this room would result in Steven becoming even more unintegrated; quite literally falling apart.

The overwhelming nature of Steven's feelings is apparent, not because he is able to tell the therapist with words but because she senses this through her attunement to him and through the feedback she gets through what Koole and Tschacher refer to as the 'synchrony' between herself and her client, a key component of the therapeutic alliance. They suggest that this can replicate the synchrony between the infant and primary care figures in that '*therapist and client have bodies that interact with each other in space and time so that communication occurs not just through words but also through bodily behaviour*' (2016:1). Through their Interpersonal Synchrony (In-Sync) model, they propose three levels on which synchrony occurs, commencing with movement synchrony embracing perceptual motor processes – our automatic movements such as breathing, eye gaze, whole body movements and our facial expressions. This can lead to the development of a shared or common language by allowing shared representations of meaning. In play therapy, this shared language is the play that the client and therapist engage in since there is no reliance on linguistics. It is this level that the therapist working with Steven is attuned to – this raw and visceral feedback or transference emanating from the unconscious.

Jordan (2015:53) suggests that for adult clients who experience the therapeutic relationship as too overwhelming, nature can be a mediator of this intensity, what he describes as nature as a transitional object. Being outside can allow the client to establish a relationship with the therapist because regardless of whether a relationship with nature pre-exists, it can be seen as a much less threatening other and allows the client to make contact with the therapist in a way which feels more manageable; less intensely intimate. When working with children, it would more generally seem to be the intensity of the feelings brought about by their early experiences which can be overwhelming rather than the intimacy of the relationship with the play therapist. However, the two are not mutually exclusive since traumatic early experiences disrupt a more usual pattern of healthy attachment and leave the child struggling. So with children, what nature might mediate instead, is the intensity of these deep inner feelings of chaos by providing a steadying hand through *concrete* examples of both stability and flexibility which they can more readily assimilate.

If as the therapist you have any doubts about the child's readiness or your own, then to move out would not be the right course of action at that point in time although at a later date you might want to revisit the idea if things change or develop.

How do I decide if I am ready?

Although we always strive to be client centred, the other important factor to consider when moving your practice outdoors is your own level of confidence in stepping beyond the playroom door and facing the possibility of having to deal with unpredictable issues. Any feelings of uncertainty you have are likely to be communicated to your client and make the whole expedition emotionally and psychologically unsafe, even if physically secure.

BAPT's good practice guidelines clearly state that:

> Play Therapists strive to benefit those with whom they work, acting in their best interests and always working within their limits of competence, training [and] experience [which] involves an obligation to use regular and on-going supervision.
>
> (BAPT 2014)

Landreth (2002), in discussing therapist self-understanding, stresses that all therapists need to be aware of and have insight into both their strengths and weaknesses since our own motivations, biases, needs or areas of potential conflict or difficulty can enter into our relationships with our clients and we need to be aware of the extent to which they do. Like Jordan above, Landreth (2002:102) suggests that this requires us to be involved in '*a process of self-exploration that will promote self-understanding*' through personal or group therapy and the supervision process. In being aware of our weaknesses, however, we must take care not to shy away from making difficult decisions, nor to allow self-doubt to lead us into thinking we are not competent therapists.

Self-reflection is essential in allowing us deeper insight into potential conflicts within our practice both at a process and personal level, but it is deeply unhelpful if it causes us to become paralysed, stuck like a rabbit in the headlights and unable to allow our practice to be dynamic and to develop. Cuschieri (2016:27), in discussing the whole issue of therapist self-doubt, reminds us that our feelings of inadequacy, our own questions and doubt, may arise from challenges on our personal beliefs and values – challenges on our 'very core'. In considering her own feelings of inadequacy, she tells us:

> I know I have a tendency to question myself, to be self-critical and to always want to do a better job. These were personal traits that were around long before I became a play therapist and are intricately linked to my personal history.

She notes how these feelings have become more acute in relation to her work as a play therapist and how she may at times assume too much responsibility for her client's emotional and psychological well-being and that both personal therapy and supervision give space to explore these issues and restore balance. She also reminds us that whilst we might expect feelings of inadequacy to arise during our training and early years as a practitioner, they also continue to follow us as we become ever more experienced. So, in recognizing the potential for our anxieties to overwhelm us, we can take positive steps to explore them and use them to enhance our work rather than allow them to hamstring us into inactivity and prohibit our creativity and development.

Our decision to move our work outside can be directly affected not only by frame and process issues and our sense of competent therapist self, but also by issues personal to us in terms of our own relationship with nature. We may not feel it is right for us for many different reasons. This is very eloquently expressed by an adolescent therapist colleague of mine:

> *My relationship to the outdoors is so important to my process ie a place of nurture, acceptance, of being and of deeply meaningful connection and of choice, that working there is almost too personal. It's me who could be easily distracted and lose my concentration on my client as the pull to my own contemplative spirituality is strong as soon as I feel the air change or hear birdsong. I'm a bit startled by the insight actually and it's also rather lovely!!*
>
> *Interestingly, I'd pick up therapeutic gardening straight away … but not in my existing garden – I'd have to set aside a garden space specifically for it. But the gardening is a concrete activity with a spiritual dimension. Being in the outdoors is a spiritual activity with a concrete dimension!*
>
> (Parker 2017)

What is meant by a 'democratic' relationship?

It is hard to find many explicit references to the idea of democracy within the play therapy relationship in the literature, although perhaps there is an implied notion of it in the term 'therapeutic alliance'; an assumed understanding that the partnership is equal. I use democratic in this context to mean a relationship where there is the best balance possible of equality and fairness given that the very nature of therapy with children and the relationship between therapist – the adult, and the client – the child, can be fraught with contradictions. How, you might ask, can we be democratic when we have already had to gain permission for the therapy to proceed from an adult who has legal responsibility for the child in question?

Having to seek consent could be seen as disempowering a child or a young person from full participation in decision making. So is there not already a tension in the notion of constructing a democratic relationship? Perhaps not, for if we bring the issues of power and control into our conscious awareness by discussion in supervision, personal therapy and with our colleagues, then we are creating the opportunity to increase our understanding of their potential effect on the dynamics of the relationship. This also enables us to be both reflective, in questioning whether or not there might be an alternative way of working which provides a more truly equal partnership, and reflexive; to consider where our issues with power and control may be rooted.

Transference issues

The majority of clients who come to play therapy have experienced some loss of control over aspects of their lives, resulting in significant feelings of disempowerment. So if the need for greater control arises, is what we are experiencing transference, a reflection of the client's unconscious process or does it sit within us? As Le Vay (2016:3) reminds us,

> To think about what we bring in with us [to a session], that which slips under the radar of our personal consciousness, inevitably reminds us to acknowledge our fallibilities … those aspects of ourselves which seep osmotically across the therapeutic boundary between self and other.

Awareness of transference, the way the child feels towards us, enables us to have a deeper insight into their inner world since we are able to understand how we are seen by them and how they react to us. In this way, we can more easily recognize how that inner world impacts on relationships they have, including that within the playroom *and* with nature (Kegerreis 2010). When we experience an emotional reaction to these transference issues, we are experiencing countertransference, feelings which arise from our own personal issues but which help us to understand the child's own unconscious emotional material. Homeyer and Morrison (2008) in discussing counter-transference, note Gil and Rubin's suggestion that countertransference issues can be more evident in relationships with children since they bring to therapy multiple aspects of themselves arising from the interactions with all those others within their world.

How do I manage interruptions?

As play therapists, we understand the importance of the integrity of the session and will always try to avoid interruptions to the session whether we are working in the playroom or beyond it. However, when we are working in the playroom, even with the best preparation and most obvious signage to tell others that a session is under way and cannot be interrupted, it happens! So the important thing about handling interruptions is that it needs to be done in a way that models an appropriate, emotionally literate response rather than one which communicates anxiety or fear to the child and suggests that such happenings are catastrophic; interruptions can be used to show the child how things do not always go as planned but that this need not be disastrous. If we also hold onto the fact that the meaning, the personal metaphor of the play is not obvious to others then we need not panic and act in a disproportionate way.

Since, through the establishment of the therapeutic relationship we know our client, we may feel we can negotiate how such interruptions will be managed if the they have sufficient capacity as described previously. If not, then as we are the therapist – the adult – we must set the limits around this, much as we would set other limits if we were in the playroom.

Landreth (2002) recognizes that despite our best efforts, there may be situations where absolute privacy and confidentiality is not possible, even in more traditional indoor settings, and notes that, in this case, we need to let the child know they may be seen or heard by others. Managing this situation may mean agreeing a special signal or word that means we stop playing if possible, and wait for those nearby to move on or allow the therapist to deal with the situation. In the playroom, if the door has a glass pane in it, then the therapist may be able to silently signal to the intruder with a shake of the head or raised hand before they open the door. If we are in a public place, we can gently repel any interruption with something playful like... *'We're having a game here and are enjoying it so much we can't stop to talk.'* If with a group, we might say ... *'We're out for the afternoon, we'll be around here for a while so you might want to find somewhere quieter!'* If people are persistent, a firmer but polite response might be needed such as... *'It would really help us if we can have the space to ourselves for this lesson so the children don't get distracted.'* The use of the term 'lesson' seems to carry a significant weight for people, perhaps because as a child they were, by and large, used to doing what a teacher asked them to do! Generally speaking, however, most people hardly notice us and those who do stop are naturally curious but move on quickly, only too pleased to see children outside enjoying themselves.

What if my client invites another child to join us?

If a child invites another who is passing to join the play, the therapist can remind the client of any agreement they might have made regarding this and emphasize that this is their special time and that they can play with others at playtime. If either child is insistent, it can become tricky, but again, we need to remember that the therapist is ultimately 'in charge' – that is, responsible for the safety of the session and that we may have to set new limits as situations arise. We might suggest we need to withdraw to the playroom or even end the session for that day. If all this is done in a quiet, calm way that lets the child know it is because the sessions are for them alone and that this is important, rather than conveying the idea that they have done something wrong and the withdrawal is a punishment, the therapeutic relationship should not be harmed.

Is running off a risk?

If we understand limit setting as an important part of the process of establishing a productive therapeutic alliance, then setting out the physical boundaries of the outdoor space becomes part of that process. Just as a child is told they need to remain in the playroom when we are working indoors, so we need to be explicit about where they can and cannot go when we move outside. Part of our assessment of whether or not we have a strong therapeutic alliance would include how the child responds to any limits and boundaries we have already set within the playroom. If they have struggled with the idea that there are things that they can't do, then the time is not right for moving outside.

When we do move outside, the space we use will need to be clearly delineated in some way (see chapter 6). If a client does decide to test the boundary, both physically and metaphorically, then we will need to reflect that we recognize being in a big space feels very different and that they may want to run but our 'job' is to keep them safe and so they can run but we need them to stay inside the agreed area. We may want to reflect that other adults in their lives might not have kept them safe but that we want to. If they do not respond to this, and really persist in breaking the boundary, we may choose to continue to work through this where we are or to take responsibility for the decision to move outside and say something like...

> *I think I got this wrong. I thought we were ready to be out here but I don't think we are. I can see it's really hard to stay in the space we agreed so I think we need to go back inside where I know you are safe. We will be able to come outside again when I know I can keep you safe.*

Transitions – using rituals and routines

In my own work, because I am aiming for the client to develop their autonomous self, whether we go outside or remain in the playroom is their decision, the above instances notwithstanding. Therefore, to start each session I generally meet them in the playroom or if I am collecting them from their classroom or other base, we usually go to the playroom first in case there are resources they want to pick up. Developing 'welcome' and 'goodbye' rituals for sessions helps to ensure a smooth transition between being indoors and moving outside, even if the ritual you have developed working in the playroom needs a slight adaption to take account of the differing environment.

Rituals have been enacted across the globe by communities and individuals to help face transitions, social changes and natural disasters and as part of spiritual beliefs and traditional healing. They have been handed down from one generation to another, providing a continuous thread that links people, places and their ways of understanding the world. Whereas ceremonies are planned, structured and focused around a particular event, rituals allow us to embark on a pathway of discovery so we open ourselves to deeper emotional exploration and the possibility of transformation. Routines, which also help to secure the child, might be likened to good habits, the things we do to make the sessions run smoothly and would include the boundaries of time, place and safe practice. For me they are the concrete, factual part of the process instigated by the therapist or the policies of the organization whereas rituals are co-constructed ways of marking our being together.

Apart from welcome and goodbye rituals, *how* sessions are ended, wherever you are working, is key in enabling the child to begin to contain their own feeling around endings and loss. Some form of countdown to the end of the session is advisable but when you are working outside, depending on whether you are planning to return to the playroom before you finish and if so, how far you are away from it, you may need to adapt it to the new circumstances. Many therapists working in nature use a mobile phone alarm to give them a signal that it is time to turn for home. Alarms can be set on 'vibrate' so that the client is unaware that it is being used, or you can tell them that when they hear it, there are x minutes of the session left so you will need to prepare to return inside.

If during the session the child says that they want to go back to the playroom, we can try to work through why they need to do this at the particular moment in time, what are they experiencing and feeling and, generally speaking, recognizing that at this particular point in time they are finding it difficult to be in the space can be enough to enable them to continue.

If they are insistent that they need to return inside, this can be explored once back in the playroom where they may feel safer to acknowledge overwhelming feelings. If the outdoor space is a distance away from the child's school or other base, we will need to reflect that if we return to the playroom, we will not be able to come back out again because of time but will be able to come to the same place for the next session. If there is a feeling of permissiveness about the movement between the indoor and outdoor space, and the child feels empowered by their choice, it is less likely that they will need to move in and out.

Parental consent

For children of primary school age, we might regard parental agreement as essential, but around the age of ten or eleven, children begin to develop the capacities needed to be regarded as competent to make decisions for themselves regarding 'treatment'. If we are working with secondary age children in a school there may be acceptance that they are competent to consent on their own behalf and we will need to use our own judgement as to whether this applies to their understanding of the therapeutic process. We will also need to be aware of the remit of any 'generic' parental permissions they may hold such as for off-site visits or counselling where this is part of pastoral support, since it may not cover everything we would want included in our own consent form for therapy in nature.

If parents are reluctant to give consent, we will need to consider what their concerns might be and if possible discuss these with them to see if additional support is needed. If we are working as part of a multi-professional group or have access to colleagues who might provide additional support, we are in a stronger position to create a climate where those with parental responsibility can feel part of the process and so lessen any anxiety. If working independently, there may still be other agencies or organizations involved with the family who can be part of a wider package of support. The following are important in ensuring effective multi-agency support:

- clarity of roles, responsibilities and timescales
- effective co-ordination – play therapy is part of an integrated process and not merely a way of fixing the child
- realistic expectations – from other professionals and parents
- regular reviews to ensure all support remains integrated and co-ordinated and to share any key themes arising from the therapy

Those who might have parental responsibility are:

- the child's mother or father
- a legally appointed guardian
- a person with an appropriate residency order
- a local authority designated to care for the child
- a local authority person with an emergency protection order

Whoever gives consent must have the capacity to do so (nhs.uk 2016). Part of our responsibility in ensuring we have consent is that it is 'informed' — that is, that those giving consent understand the therapeutic process and the boundaries and limitations around it so that expectations are realistic and do not put pressure on the child, the therapist or the process.

When seeking consent for therapy, this usually goes hand in hand with gathering personal details about the child although the extent of this information may vary from therapist to therapist. Most professional organizations will offer guidance on both processes but whether we are working indoors or in an outdoor space, there are some crucial pieces of information we will need such as:

- emergency contact details including GP
- medical concerns including allergies
- cultural needs
- any specific behaviours to be aware of
- any additional learning or personal care needs
- dietary needs if appropriate to activities

When we are working outside, there are occasions when we might need to make physical contact with a child such as hold a hand to help them negotiate an obstacle or pull off a wet welly. These actions will take place in an appropriate context and are part of our duty of care, but we would be advised to note them on the consent form so that parents or the referring agency are aware of them and any concerns they might raise can be discussed at the outset of the therapy. A good rule of thumb about what to include in the consent form would be anything that you feel you need to raise awareness of that would not generally occur in the playroom including appropriate clothing and any special resources you might be using such as a campfire.

...and finally

How outdoor places are incorporated into play therapy sessions is a matter of choice for each therapist, depending on the orientation of their work and their own relationship with nature. Some therapists have moved into the outdoors with ease, some have decided it is not for them and some work in a contained space such as a withy structure or small summer house within an outdoor space. Some play therapists have chosen to only work in an outdoor space such as a woodland or beach setting and do not access an indoor space at all. But once you have started to think that nature may have something to offer the process that is play therapy, I suspect it will not be long before you start to make your way through the playroom door with your client. Working in nature is, as Jordan notes, a unique and different setting from the room. In this respect, it requires us to review many aspects of our practice and to find new ways of being with ourselves and our clients in the presence of nature as a co-therapist and to acknowledge '*humans and nature as co-existent and interdependent, mergent and emergent in relational processes*' (2015:24).

References

BAPT (2014) *Play Therapy Core Competences: Practice Skills(29)*. Available from: www.bapt.info/play-therapy/play-therapy-core-competences/ [Accessed 12th November 2016]

Chown, A. (2014) *Play Therapy: Taking Play Therapy out of the Playroom and into Natural Environments*. London: Jessica Kingsley Publishers

Cuschieri, E. (2016) Can I really do this? An exploration of therapist self-doubt. In Le Vay, D. and Cuschieri, E. (eds) *Challenges in the Theory and Practice of Play Therapy*. Abingdon: Routledge, pp. 18–37

Holden, S. (2017) Email sent to Alison Chown, 9th January

Homeyer, L. E. and Morrison, M. O. (2008) Play therapy: Practice, issues and trends. *American Journal of Play*, Fall, 210–228. Available from: www.journalofplay.org/sites/www.journalofplay.org/files/pdf-articles/1-2-article-play-therapy.pdf [Accessed 23rd November 2016]

Jordan, M. (2015) *Nature and Therapy: Understanding Counselling and Psychotherapy in Outdoor Spaces*. Hove: Routledge

Kegerreis, S. (2010) *Psychodynamic Counselling with Children and Young People: An Introduction*. England: Palgrave MacMillan

Koole, S. L. and Tschacher, W. (2016) Synchrony in psychotherapy: A review and an integrative framework for the therapeutic alliance. *Hypothesis and Theory*. Available from: doi: 10.3389/fpsyg.2016.00862.2016.06.14 published 14th June 2016 [Accessed 23rd October 2016]

Landreth, G. (2002) *The Art of the Relationship* (2nd edition). Hove: Brunner–Routledge

Le Vey, D. (2016) To be or not to be? The therapeutic use of self within child-centred play therapy. In Le Vay, D. and Cuschieri, E. (eds) *Challenges in the Theory and Practice of Play Therapy*. Abingdon: Routledge, pp. 1–17

nhs.uk (2016) *Consent to Treatment – Children and Young People*. Available from: www.nhs.uk/Conditions/Consent-to-treatment/Pages/Children-under-16.aspx [Accessed 15th November 2016]

Oaklander, V. (1988) *Windows to Our Children*. New York: The Gestalt Journal Press

Parker, J. (2017) Email sent to Alison Chown. 17th January

Wilson, K., Kendrick, P. and Ryan, V. (1992) *Play Therapy: A Non-directive Approach for Children and Adolescents*. London: Bailliere and Tindall

Chapter 6

Places to go, spaces to use – meeting the elements

When we talk of the elements, we tend to think of naturally occurring phenomena, particularly rain, wind, sunshine and other aspects of the weather. However, the concept of 'five elements' is common to many cultures and is concerned with:

- earth
- air
- fire
- water
- spirit or quintessence, the fifth element

In Ancient Greece, the first four were pre-scientific concepts concerned with both the nature and qualities of substances and the complexity of all matter, with the fifth, spirit or 'aether' as it was known then, added by Aristotle.

In Buddhism, the four elements of earth, air, fire and water help us to understand what we are really feeling and so begin to liberate ourselves from suffering. Earth symbolizes both solidity and inertia, air expansion and vibration, fire heat or energy and water cohesion. These four elements form the primary group of the eight 'kalapas' categories of both mind and matter with the secondary group comprised of colour, taste, smell and nutrient.

Chinese medicine considers the five elements to be concerned with processes and change; interactions and relationships, with our health being a harmonious balance of all five. They differ slightly from the Western elements, being instead, wood, fire, metal, water and earth. Each has a different and distinct characteristic, with wood symbolizing benevolence, fire propriety, metal righteousness, water wisdom and earth fidelity or honesty.

In Paganism, earth is the ultimate feminine element whose energy is grounding. She is symbolic of nurture, solidity and enduring strength. She is what we might call 'Mother Earth'. Air is both the breath and soul of life. It can transport – blowing away trouble and carrying our thoughts to those in far away places. Fire is symbolic of the sun. It has feminine purifying energy that is both forceful and powerful. It can be both creator and destroyer, can heal us or cause us harm. Water has feminine energy, and is symbolic of the womb. It is concerned with our subconscious, with our dreams and emotions and symbolizes passion.

Quintessence, or spirit, the fifth energy also known as 'akasha' from Sanskrit is considered to be beyond the material world, to be everywhere and yet nowhere. It has no defined location and is said to allow us to be open to something bigger than ourselves. In relation to play therapy in the outdoors, in nature, this resonates with the idea of the democratic space, that which belongs to neither but to both. Perhaps also it suggests that in not having a 'fixed' space, one that is surrounded by solid walls, we facilitate greater openness for our clients which gives rise to more real and deeper connections in their relationship with their own self, with others and with the environment around them, with nature. The other elements combine aspects of both nature and our own biological and emotional life processes, so providing us with a bridge between outer and inner worlds. It is the symbolism and metaphors they offer us, both as themselves and through the interactions they have with each other and with the land around us, that makes working in the outdoors a more powerful experience for our clients.

This section of the book is about some of the different environments you might work in and some of the elements within them. As you will have read in the introduction to this book, because I work non-directively, I do not use any kind of session-by-session programme. The sessions have a structure in that we will have a 'welcome' and 'farewell' ritual, particular to each client or client group, but beyond that I work with whatever comes up. When I am working with a group, however, there are occasions when an activity is helpful, particularly at the start of a session to bring everyone together or to re-ground the children if they have been working at a deep level. Breathing and relaxation activities can form part of either your welcome or farewell rituals or both. The child/ren are free to take resources from the playroom and appendix 4 contains a list of additional materials you might gather.

The activities that follow are some of those I use and if you are stepping out for the first time, they may help both you and your clients to familiarize yourselves with working in nature and relax into 'being' together. However, most of the available research, discussion in supervision and many anecdotes from parents and grandparents tell us that when children are outdoors, they really do just get on and play. We do not need to direct them any more than we do in the playroom. They know what they need to do.

You may already know some of the activities, you may even use them yourself. Games and activities like these are handed down from generation to generation, from person to person and across many clubs, institutions and organizations. When we come across them, we use them and often adapt them to suit the individual or group we are working with. Some of the activities outlined here have arisen as a result of being in the moment with a client or group and may have come from the child/ren themselves. Use them as you will. Adapt or change them if you need to – they are owned by no-one!

It is not possible to cover all the places you might use, but by looking at some of the elements that might feature, some of the amazing sights, sounds, smells, shapes and textures that nature presents us with and how they can be seen as both symbolic of and metaphorical for our lives, I hope you will feel confident to step out and experience nature in your play therapy sessions. The narrative passages in italics come from within me and will prompt you to think about some of the metaphors they offer. You can read them to yourself, or to your clients, and change or adapt them in any way you need in order to take account of your and the child/ren's own experiences and age.

But... before you step out

Once you are thinking of stepping beyond the playroom door and working in nature, there are some things to reflect on to prepare yourself which you may have already considered in supervision. If not, give them some quiet thought first.

Are you ready to leave the playroom?

I cannot emphasize the importance of this enough. As we have discussed, our own readiness is equally as important as our client's in order that the therapeutic relationship, the container for work in nature, is not compromised in any way by our feelings of anxiety, fear or apprehension. Whether you are ready to offer your clients an outdoor space or are still a little undecided, you can reflect on your own relationship with nature, if you have not already done so, in the following time-honoured way.

Getting to know the place – the 'sit spot'

In chapter 4 we discussed the idea of a sense of place, the meaning a place may have for us or that we give it. Before working in a particular outdoor environment with our clients, it is important that we get to know the space, to be acquainted with the natural life that exists in it, to be aware of nature and all that she is offering. The sit spot was a place where a hunter would go to sit, observe and wait for his prey to appear and familiarize himself with the landscape, flora and fauna. Those of us who want to connect with nature for a very different reason, can use the sit spot to allow ourselves to be still and to be open to connecting with nature with all of our senses. Gietz (2014) suggests that a sit spot should be close to home, have nature and be solitary and safe. We may be working in school grounds, in a nearby wood or forest school, in a local park or urban setting or on the beach, but wherever our space is, we can find a sit spot.

To be solitary does not mean to be isolated from others, but to be fully focused on our own purpose rather than being distracted by others around us. The sit spot is a place to really get to know nature, to observe the changes brought on by the weather and the seasons, to know the animals, birds and insects that are present, to see the plants and trees and to hear whatever noise is around. We are encouraged to go to the sit spot every day, but if this is not possible, we can at least get to know the place it is in different weather, seasons and times of the day. So get to know the space where you will work. Sit in solitude and open your senses to all that is there. Think also about any meaning the place has for you so you are clear when you are working with a client which issues may arise from within you and which from within the child.

If you are going to use a variety of locations, selecting a sit spot in each of them and visiting regularly is not necessarily possible but it's important to take time to visit each location on several different occasions, at different times of the day and in different weathers. Be aware of the changes that will occur for example after heavy rain when streams and rivers can flood or run much faster or ground can become boggy and inaccessible. This will all feed into any risk benefit analysis you do so making notes or taking photographs is always helpful. Identify the entry and exit spot for each space so that using these becomes part of your ritual at the beginning and end of the session.

If you are working with clients who have any additional and specific needs, or mobility or other impairments, is the site accessible and if not, can it be made so with some adaptions?

The Bridge Project was run at a pupil referral unit for young people aged 11–16 who attended full-time after having been excluded from school or part-time if they were at risk of exclusion. The project provided for a group of four boys aged 11–12 years to have individual play therapy in the morning in the centre's therapy room and a group session in various outdoor locations in the afternoon, accompanied by a male teacher, a female teacher/therapist, a teaching assistant and the play therapist. During the afternoon visits the adult/child ratio was 1:1, such was the general volatility of the individuals.

The location for each week's visit was selected by the therapist according to the weather, tides and the changing needs of the group arising from the issues which were coming out of the individual sessions. Sometimes, the volatility of the group suggested more open space was needed where they could be with an adult but without the close proximity of the others. On more harmonious occasions, a walk through the woods together with time to play in the stream offered opportunities for more relaxed individual contact with each boy whilst building the sense of group belonging.

To use a sit spot as suggested above was not possible since the locations were some way from both the staff homes and the centre. However, the therapist and one of teachers visited each location that was likely to be used in order to risk assess in line with the centre's policy and to familiarize themselves with the nature of the location in its broadest sense, both the nature that existed there and the elemental nature in respect of shelter spots and likely weather impact. Locations included two beaches, one open and sandy and located on the edge of a seaside town, the other more isolated and strewn with rocks and boulders, woods with a river running through them, open grassland with flood management watercourses and sluice gates adjacent to an estuary, a small play park and a leisure park with boating lake and play areas.

'Take only pictures, leave only footprints, kill only time'

This well-known phrase, the source of which is not easily identifiable, has several different forms, but this version sums up the approach we need to adopt when working in nature. It can be used as part of basic limit setting when you are outdoors and 'kill only time' relates not just to animals, insect and bird life, but to plants, flowers and trees.

When working in nature, we always aim to leave each location as we have found it and picking plants and flowers, or greenery from trees, breaking branches, or other destructive activities is discouraged. If we are building a shelter, or image making, anything safe that is already lying on the ground – not growing! – may be used and this might mean we have to bring some suitable materials with us. Anything we use from the site needs to be returned to its place before we leave. This practice, whilst safeguarding the space, also helps the child/ren to become well acquainted with what is natural to a place and what might have been brought there by human visitors. Remember to make it clear that anything that does not naturally belong in the space you are using but that has been left by others – human or animal – is not for touching! Look critically at the space you will be working in and consider any other essential limitations that you will need to outline with the child/ren.

We can go outside...

The next thing to consider is how you will introduce the idea of an outside space or working in nature to your clients. If you are starting in the playroom, be clear about how you will both know that the child is ready and how you will reach the agreement to move outside. Will you show the child the space when you first meet them much as you would introduce the playroom to them or simply tell them the space is out there and visit it if they ask to see it? If you intend to only work in an outdoor space, will you take the child/ren there for a short introductory visit or meet them there for the first session? If you are using several locations, how will you decide on which one and will it be a joint decision or solely yours to make? You will also need to have considered if returning to the playroom, or moving in and out of it, during a session is an option, and if there are any limits which need to apply to this. What will happen if you are working off-site and your client wants to come back to base? Will time allow you to return to your outdoor space or will you finish the session in the playroom?

And don't forget to pay mind to the issues of handwashing and toileting as this is an aspect of being away from the playroom which some clients (and therapists!) can be very concerned about, including those from different social and religious cultures or those who have additional personal care needs. (See appendix 2 – Health and Safety advice.) Once outside, we also need to remember that our clients may not always be as comfortable being in nature as we are so it is important to keep checking in with them so that physical discomforts like being very cold or hot or having wet feet can be attended to.

Shelter spot

Provided the child/ren you are working with have warm clothes and good waterproofs or hats and sunscreen, being out in all weathers is not problematic. **What does restrict going outside is if the ground underfoot is slippery, there are very high winds which might cause damage, particularly if you are working in woods or the forest, or there is a thunderstorm.** Once you are familiar with the space you will be using, you will be able to identify a shelter spot, somewhere that offers some protection from the elements and to where you can retreat if necessary. It may also be possible to construct a shelter and this is an activity you can do with the child/ren as part of your first session outside or as the need arises. Shelter is needed not only from rain and wind but also from the sun. On the following pages, we will discuss the easiest way to build a simple shelter. If it is not possible to construct a shelter you can always agree to retreat indoors!

The 'nest' – a secure base

In chapter 2 we discussed how the mother figure provides a secure base from which the child can venture forth into the world. When we are working outside, the therapeutic relationship we have made with our client/s provides that safety and security but I have found having a physical base is helpful. When working with a group, it provides a focus for coming together and is a great place for storytelling.

I like to call this base our 'nest' and children seem to understand its function and significance from this term. It is the place where we can gather to start, leave our resources and return to finish. The nest can be as simple as a blanket or piece of plastic on the ground to a more complex den structure. You can use natural materials or provide old cardboard boxes, lengths of fabric or a tarpaulin or plastic sheeting. In each of the following sections, some ideas for nest construction are given.

Picture 'map' books

These are small books (15 × 10 cm) of spiral-bound photographs of particular objects or points on a walk or pathway that can be used as way finders. The spiral binding keeps them together but allows for the pages to easily be flipped over. Alternatively you can punch a hole in the top left-hand corner of each picture and thread them onto strong string or twine or secure with an old key ring (see fig 6:1).

Fig 6:1 Spiral-bound 'map book' – tailor-made for each different place

They enable children to find their way without having to read instructions or a traditional map. They do, however, prepare the ground for using Ordnance Survey maps. You can make them by choosing permanent or seasonal things such as signposts, large rocks or boulders, buildings, unusual trees or shrubs, fallen logs, hills and hollows or views. If you use seasonal things such as particular flowers, make sure you change the book as the seasons progress!

Print off the photographs, laminate them and bind so that pages can be flipped over. They can be used by individual children or pairs to encourage working together. They engender a sense of equality since even though the therapists may be familiar with the path, she does not have to lead the way.

Species identification books

There are many commercially produced books but making one that is specific to the location/s you are using is an alternative (see fig 6:2). As with the map books, they are made up of laminated photographs, spirally bound but with the name and habitat details on the reverse of each picture (do this before lamination!). Once again these pave the way for the use of the commercially produced ones which tend to be more comprehensive but

Fig 6:2 A tailor-made specimen identification book, ring-bound for ease of handling

therefore not as easy to refer to for children with poor reading skills and little or no patience.

A word about litter

The space you are using needs to be as clear of litter and other potentially harmful debris as possible. If you are working in school grounds this may be taken care of at the end of each day by the caretaker or site manager. If you are working in a public space, there may be litter collection by the council at some point and your 'sit spot' observation may well tell you of this, but you will need to visit your site on the day you plan to use it to carefully remove any rubbish or hazardous material as part of your risk/benefit process. Having said this, always keep your eyes open as you are playing together for anything you might have missed or that appears between your checking of and using of the space.

A word of warning – Always use a litter picker or appropriate protective gloves and avoid touching anything that might cause you harm such as chemical containers and sharp or corroded metal objects. If these are present, the space is not suitable for your use.

Halfway houses

If you want to work outside but feel you still want access to a small permanent or semi-permanent contained space within the outdoor environment, there are a number of structures I have seen being used which can also be adapted to make shelters:

- a small withy dome
- a tent (fig 6:3)
- a large tent which can be opened at either end (fig 6:4)
- a camping gazebo
- a parachute suspended from a tree and anchored at points near the ground
- a small grass-covered corrugated arc (fig 6:5)
- a small beach or fishing shelter
- a den constructed from old pallets and tarpaulins
- a garden shed
- a playhouse

The activities that follow are the ones I use if children need to familiarize themselves with working outside so that they feel safe and can trust the therapeutic relationship in the changed environment. Suffice it to say I generally find that we just carry on as before and I don't need to offer the more structured activities. If you are working with children with physical or learning impairments, you can adapt most of the activities to their needs.

Fig 6:3 The 'igloo' tent

Fig 6:4 The 'big' tent

Fig 6:5 The little tunnel – a small pig arc

Water – beaches and inland watercourses

Water, water everywhere… in the sea, in rivers and streams, in fountains, springs and lakes, in marshy ground and puddles on the road, in our taps, showers and baths and in our bodies. Water is the giver of life and children generally love it! They love splashing in it, running through it, stamping in it, hurling it skywards from buckets, rolling in it, swimming in it, damming it in streams and following it along river banks and the edges of brooks. Some are scared of it. It offers us much potential therapeutically for there can be great metaphor in water. '*Swimming, like life, is a solitary act. Life, like water, is something you have to move through. Water is life giving but it can also take you under*' (Bennett 2012).

In the Christian tradition of baptism, water cleanses, washes away sin and facilitates a changed person who accepts Christ into their life. As a small child I remember vividly a baptism in the river Avon, where the pastor of the local Baptist church waded into the shallower waters at the edge of the river in his wellington boots, and gently lowered a woman backwards into the water until she was immersed. I remember wondering if she was going to drown and the relief that 'flooded' over me when she emerged to applause from the congregation on the bank. I didn't really make sense of what had happened and my parents' explanation of her having accepted Jesus into her life only raised the

Fig 6:6 Sand and pebble beach

question from me of where they were going to live! But the memory stayed fresh in my mind and in my body for weeks and I could feel how cold it must have been, how it must have felt for the pastor when the water went over the top of his wellies – a sensation I was very familiar with, how the water would go up the woman's nose unless she pinched it close and the feeling in my belly when I thought she might drown.

Water is the giver of life, but perhaps because around 60% of our bodies are water, there is something more which draws us towards it.

> Water is one of the most crucial elements in the Persian garden, and we can state that gardens would be meaningless without it. Garden applications use water with its various abilities such as life, brightness, cleanliness, light, inertia, and motion, which bring forward numerous feelings in the human soul and enhance mental comfort. Also, its various running structures, such as basins, streams, water creeks, and fountains, provide mental comfort and technical functions.
>
> (Fekete and Haidari 2015)

Water is not only essential to life but also to the quality of our lives. It is a powerful natural force that can wreak havoc and destruction like the tsunami, or can lie still and quiet like the flat calm sea. Rivers and streams are like the flow of our lives, sometimes easy and free-running, sometimes blocked by boulders and debris so that a new path must be taken which finds a way around the obstacles. Sometimes the watercourse is rich with life – weeds and plants, animals and fishes – and at other times it is polluted, murky and dank, or nearly dried up so that nothing flourishes in it, on it or even near it.

On the beach

We live on an island surrounded by the sea that is relentlessly restless, ever moving, rolling in and out like breath on the wind. Sometimes that breath is gentle and sometimes wilder and full of pent-up feeling. For many people, the beach is the place to head when the sun is shining and the prospect of a day doing nothing of any great import is entirely pleasurable. But what does the sea mean to us? It has associations with mythical creatures like the Kraken and it has been home to pirates, both real and fictional, to the navies of the world and host to some of the most demanding boat races of our time. Men and women have sailed on it, rowed across it and swum in it, some for pleasure, some for sport, some to escape danger. Many have lost their lives to it, some whilst trying to save others. And in our present time, thousands of refugees have paid to ride in poorly equipped, leaky and dangerously overcrowded vessels crewed by those interested only in their money and who generally abandon them to their fate long before they reach land, which for too many is death by drowning.

And yet, the other face of the sea is a benign one – one that entices us into her waves to surf, or onto her gentle waters to swim and frolic on hot days. Our island coastline is so varied; from wide sandy beaches with breakers rolling in to sheer cliff faces that are rooted directly into the sea; from soft, silken sand to large pebbles and boulders; from crowded beaches where we perch at high tide like cormorants on a rock to vast stretches of sand that see only a few visitors and where you can run wild and free, shrieking into the wind or rolling over and over in the sand.

Working near water is really important to me, perhaps because of the constant movement and the fact that it touches all of our senses. We can see it, hear it, touch it, smell it and taste it from clean sources. We can immerse ourselves in it and under it. I particularly love working on the beach; for me it is both richly metaphorical and symbolic:

> *Come down to the beach my friend and walk barefoot upon the sand. Slip off your shoes and wiggle your toes into the hot then cold fine grains of yester-years' rocks and cliffs. Sit awhile upon its warmth and sift it gently through*

your fingers. Let it pour over your hands, trickle between them and fall gently back to join the other millions upon millions of tiny flecks beneath you.

Lift your head and look to the horizon across sparkling salty water where the sun dances brightly. Do you ever feel like dancing? Do you want to leap and whirl and step out wildly? Can you show me how you dance?

If we move further along the beach, the grains grow bigger, become small stones and pebbles that make dancing more difficult. Move further on again and there are large pebbles and rocks which block our way, over which we must scramble, having a less sure hold on the pathway we are taking. But look carefully as you walk for you can find treasures – shells, curiously shaped pebbles, colourful stones or frosty pieces of glass worn smooth by the rolling of the sea and the rubbing of the sand and pebbles. You can keep these safe, find a place to put them where you know they will stay and use them to tell a story or create an image.

Down at the water's edge, today the tide washes gently over the sand and stones. Its rhythm can match our resting heartbeat, marking our existence with its barely audible swish, swish. Can you feel your heart beating? Put your hand here.

Come another day, when the wind is wild and clouds darken the sky and the sea will crash against the shore, spitting white foam high against the rocks, angry and punishing, spilling over everything in its path. Like our anger, it is wilful and untameable, driven from a dark place deep inside. I wonder if you ever feel like the wild sea, huge and angry, sweeping past everything in your pathway, unable to bear the great big feeling bursting inside you.

Can you draw the feeling on the sand? What does it look like? How big is it? Let's mark its path together, but you show me the way.

Getting to know the place

Even if the beach is familiar to the child/ren, it is always worth taking time to get to know the space. Spend a few minutes just standing and looking. Remind them of any limitations you have in mind. Mark the 'territory' you will be using with them, either by using a rope or by sighting any natural or constructed marker points like steps, rocks, walls, wooden sea defences and buildings. On a sandy beach you can draw the area but be aware that the lines may disappear if they are walked on or run across. You might decide to use a rope for a few sessions until they are really familiar with the space, and then use other marker points.

Use species identification books to familiarize the child/ren with what lives on the beach. Rather than collecting things, move around the area, identifying as you go. Look at what lives in the sea, at the tide line and on the beach. Talk about what can and can't be collected if you are going to do some art later in the session.

Health and safety pointers

- Always check the weather! Benign streams and rivers can turn into raging torrents during, and for some considerable time after, heavy rain due to the run-off from higher ground. Dry ground can become saturated and boggy so always plan a safe path away from potentially difficult areas. This is why it is important to spend time in getting to know the space you will be using in different weathers.
- If you are using beaches, know the times of both high and low water. At low water, deep muddy areas or unstable sand may appear which will need to be avoided and you need to know how far up the beach the highest tide reaches. Plan for an escape route off the beach to be on the safe side.
- Children love rock pools and love seeing what they contain. When moving over rocks, or other potentially slippery surfaces, use *the three point rule*. Our points are our hands and feet. Always keep three in contact with the ground so two feet and one hand or two hands and one foot. This gives good stability and helps to prevent slips and falls. If the child does slip, they have good contact with the ground to steady themselves to avoid serious injury. However, if the surfaces are very slippery, especially if they are also steep, you might decide to move to another area and avoid them altogether.
- Many children like dogs, some don't. Most dog owners are fairly responsible but some are definitely not. Not all dogs are friendly, whatever their owner thinks! My 'rule' about dogs is: if one approaches, the child/ren quietly stand still, put their hands in their coat pockets or fold their arms and wait until the dog has gone past. ***Dogs are not for patting unless you really know them.***

Building a nest

The simplest nest is a hollow in the sand as deep as you want make it, lined with plastic and a blanket. You can build a sand wall around all or part of it to give a little more protection.

Using tent awning poles, twine and a small tarpaulin or sheet of plastic will give you some shelter from the rain, or in hot weather use a light blanket or piece of fabric. If you are with a group and don't have any awning poles, the children can take it in turns to act as a tent pole by standing on either side of the nest to support the canopy.

You can build a nest in a similar way on a shingle or pebble beach. However, if you want to build a low wall you will need a tarpaulin or larger sheet of plastic which provides a good overlap so you can secure the material used for the wall safely to stop pebbles rolling in onto the child/ren (see fig 6:7).

Alternatively, use one of the small, lightweight portable beach shelters that are available, weighting it down with sand or stones to stop it blowing away. If you use the 'pop-up' variety, make sure you are familiar with the way to get it back into the bag. Many an hour has been lost by those wrestling to do so in a stiff breeze!

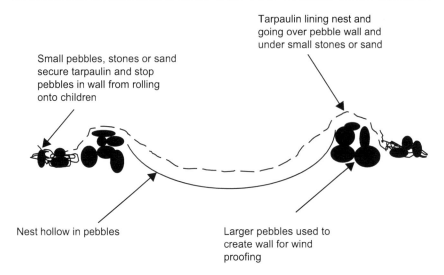

Tarpaulin lining nest and going over pebble wall and under small stones or sand

Small pebbles, stones or sand secure tarpaulin and stop pebbles in wall from rolling onto children

Nest hollow in pebbles

Larger pebbles used to create wall for wind proofing

Fig 6:7 How to construct a pebble beach nest

A group of children were working with their therapist on the beach. They had made a 'nest' in a hollow in the sand and had lined it with blankets. They created a story together about how the puppets they had brought with them had all been on their first visit to the seaside. The puppets had had a grand day out, playing in the waves, building sandcastles, playing games and eating ice-cream and chips, and hadn't noticed how late it was getting. As the sun began to set, the puppets realized they had missed the last bus home. What would they do? They would have to spend the night on the beach. But a storm was brewing and it was threatening to rain. The children decided to build the puppets a 'nest' each so that they would have shelter and so would be warm and dry. While they were doing this, they chatted to the therapist about how it felt to be safe inside the house when there was bad weather outside. They imagined what the puppets might be feeling being away from their home and family and this led on to talk of times when the children themselves had been away from home or had not been safe and how this had made them feel. Being with the elements in the environment where the puppets would have to stay overnight enabled the children to really feel the feeling of being stuck on the beach and unable to get home; of feeling unsafe but contained by the therapeutic relationship. This allowed deeper access of their own embodied life metaphors, described in chapter 2.

The contrast between the light side and the shadow side of nature is perhaps one of the most powerful aspects for children. Many of my clients experience overwhelming feelings of anger and rage. They feel out of control and uncontrollable, a frightening place to be, and will often tell the adults working in their schools... '*you can't stop me ... you can't make me ... I'm not listening to you...*' They are letting them know that they feel powerful, unstoppable, and yet at the same time are crying out for those adults *to* stop them, to contain them and make them feel safe again. The loss of control is often followed by crying and desolation. They are lost in the dance between two extremes and trying to get them to see and feel that there is a place between these two, a place where there is an equilibrium, can be extremely hard.

The sea offers us a concrete and visible metaphor for this; one day the sea is rough, angry and pounding, frightening in its intensity, and the next it can be flat calm, almost lifeless. But on many days, it runs in between these two states, rolling onto the sand with gentle waves we can play in, waves that have power and life but which allow us to be in them and with them without them bowling us over, symbolic of our potential ability to be with others in a way that does not frighten or overpower them.

Activities

Relaxation: On a day when the sea is in this state, sit or stand and watch it for a few minutes. Breathe in the rhythm of the waves rolling in and out. Listen to the sound they make. On sand it is soft, sometimes barely audible, yet it is still there. On pebbles the noise is louder but the action is still rhythmic and rolling. Lie back on the beach, side by side. Can you tell when a wave is coming in? How do you know? Close your eyes, and put your arms by your sides and keep them flat on the ground. As the wave comes in use your fingers to scoop sand or pebbles into your hand and release them as the wave goes out. You might find you have built a little pile after a while.

Now put your hands on your belly where your solar plexus or centre is. Breathe in as the wave breaks and out as it rolls away. Breathe in deeply so that your hands move up as you breathe in and then down as you breathe out.

Make an ocean drum: Fill a medium-sized box or tin with sand, shingle or small pebbles and see if you can recreate the noise you hear. You can take this home and when you begin to feel cross, lie or sit somewhere quiet if you can. Close your eyes and picture yourself lying on the beach and think how calm you felt. Use your drum to remind you of the rhythm of the sea. Breathe deeply with it ... in and out ... in and out ... in and out until you start to relax. Keep your drum somewhere safe.

When the sea is stormy, it has a huge amount of energy which it discharges in crashing waves. If it didn't release this energy it could become overpowering and destructive. Being active helps us to release adrenaline and cortisol which builds up inside us when we are frightened, distressed or angry. If we are in danger, the energy it creates can help us to get clear, but it is not helpful energy to have inside us otherwise. When we feel it, we can use it to help us get active. Then we can begin to feel more settled again.

Playing 'chicken' in the waves (not big ones!): As the wave goes out, follow it a little way towards the sea and wait for the next one to come in. Stay as long as you can in that place, until you think the wave will get you, then run back up the beach to stay dry. This is easier if you have wellies but not nearly so much fun!

Scuttle like a crab: Sit on the ground, with your arms behind you, hands on the ground. Have your feet out in front but with knees bent. Lift your bottom up and try to move sideways like a crab! If you get really good at this, take it in turns to play follow my leader. If you are part of a group, you can play crab football!

Sharks and minnows: (A version of 'Grandmother's footsteps' or 'What's the time Mr Wolf'.) One of you is the shark and one the minnow. The minnow 'swims' around by taking a meandering path around the beach while the shark follows. When the minnow stops to feed, the shark must stop still. As they go to feed, the minnow looks behind them. If the shark is moving they swop places. If the shark is still, they carry on until the minnow catches the shark out. In a group, it is played like 'Mr Wolf' with the shark turning her back on all the minnows who start some distance away and try to creep up to reach the shark, wiggling in the manner of a minnow. If they are moving or making any sound when the shark turns, they have to freeze and stay where they are. The other minnows continue. The first minnow to reach the shark takes their place and everyone starts again. A good activity for learning physical and affect regulation.

Beach creations: The beach is just a great big sand tray and a great place for art since sand and pebbles can be manipulated in many ways, including 'rubbing out' and starting again. Gather anything safe that you can see on the beach such as driftwood, dried seaweed, bits of old rope, unusual stones and shells to create a picture. If you are in a group then you might want to make a picture together to show what you have done during the session or how you felt being out on the beach.

And finally, a sandy beach provides an even deeper sand box than the one used by McCarthy and described in chapter 1. It can offer a truly immersive and transformative experience as illustrated by the following case study:

The play therapist was working on the beach with a group of four boys aged between eleven and twelve during their eighth session in the outdoors. They were together on a wide, flat sandy beach, accompanied by three other members of staff from the school the boys attended. The boys spent the first quarter of an hour or so digging somewhat aimlessly in the sand before one went off down to the water's edge with one of the staff members. Two of the remaining three boys, who were close friends, shouted 'Bury us in the sand, go on, bury us. Make it a real big deep hole!'

The therapist and teacher started to dig a hole and the two boys joined in, jumping in now and again to check the depth. When it was deep enough for them to sit in with their heads just above the edge of the hole, they got into a large plastic 'bivvy bag' to keep themselves dry and hopped down into the hole shouting 'Cover us right up!' The bag came over their heads so the therapist rolled it down below their faces and everyone around the hole filled it in again until it reached the boys' shoulders. Only their heads were visible! They were shrieking with delight and laughing, shouting 'It's heavy, really heavy. We can't move anything. Help us out now!' They tried to struggle free but were stuck fast. The others started to dig them out while the boys continued shouting and laughing. As the sand was cleared, they began to be able to move and wriggle, squirming and straining to lever themselves out. Then one of them remarked 'Ooooo! It's just like being born again, like a baby popping out!' They continued squirming and wriggling and saying 'I'm a baby being born, mama, mama. Help me out, help me out.' When they finally emerged, giggling and laughing, they shouted 'We've been born again, look we're babies' and spent the last minutes of the session crawling on the sand saying 'gag ga goo goo, I want my bottle, I need my nappy changed' and crawling away from the 'Mum and Dad', the therapist and teacher, saying they were being naughty babies! In the minibus on the way back, the play on the beach gave rise to chatter about early childhood memories, very poignant for one of the boys whose father had left when he was only a toddler and who sat quietly looking out of the window.

As they travelled, contained by the relationship with the therapist and the 'walls' of the minibus, he was able to acknowledge how sad he felt about his Dad leaving but also how angry he was with him. When the therapist asked him where in his body he felt his anger, he pointed to his belly 'There, in the same place I got a funny feeling when we were stuck in the sand.' The therapist reflected that when he was stuck and couldn't do anything, or take any action, he felt panicky in his belly. She wondered if that was how he had felt when his Dad left home. The boy said it was an angry feeling, like when he got stuck with his work and he shouted at his teacher even though he liked him. The therapist helped to reframe this:

Oh, so you get a funny angry feeling in your belly when you get stuck, like the feeling you might have had when your Dad left and you couldn't do anything about it – then you shout at your teacher even though you like him. It's like that sometimes, we can both like and not like some people at the same time.

The boy was quiet for a few minutes, staring out of the window again, then he looked at the therapist, said 'Maybe!' and joined in a game with the other boys.

Streams, rivers and other watercourses

Let's follow the stream that we meet as we walk down this track, the silver thread of water that meanders its way across the field and into the wood. Our path through life can be like a stream, not going in a straight line, taking an easy route, but wandering this way and that, working its way past obstacles and blockages but always finding a way to go.

Sometimes it disappears from sight and we have to stand still and listen carefully to hear its gentle voice calling us. Then we might shriek with delight, or call out to the others when we find it again. I wonder if you remember listening for someone's voice and the feeling you had when you heard them?

Our stream is small here, maybe we can jump to the other side? Perhaps we need to help each other – can you take my hand so I know I will be safe when I'm crossing over it? If you want to run on ahead and find where it goes, can you wait when you get to the big tree with branches that reach into the water so we don't lose each other?

Inland watercourses suggest different metaphors to the sea. They are like the pathways we travel on in life. They can meander gently, flow swiftly, rush hither and thither over rocks and boulders, tumble over waterfalls and weirs and spread themselves wide as they look to join the sea. Their pathway may not always be easy, but water keeps moving, whether it is in a river or a stream or down a windowpane, it keeps going. For me there is something here about trusting ourselves to keep going, even when the path we are taking becomes difficult to negotiate. It expresses our ability to be resilient, even though that resilience may ebb and flow. We need to trust ourselves to be able to find a way to negotiate the difficulties.

Activities

Can you spot ... hear or smell? You will need to have visited the site several times prior to taking the child/ren there for this activity. This is similar to the more traditional treasure hunt where children collect things on a list but nothing needs to be picked up. Take a walk along the side of the watercourse and see what you can see, hear and smell. Use the example in appendix 5 to design a 'Can you spot?' list of your own. If you are working with a group, you can ask each child to find a sit spot and then make a list of their own and swop with each other.

Dry welly crossing: If you are working with a group for the first time, this activity can help you assess the level of cohesion and co-operation within the group. You will need to have found a shallow crossing point in the watercourse where the level is slightly variable but not too deep for the children to wade in. You will need a walking pole or strong stick and some waterproof tape – gaffer tape works well. On the stick, measure where the top of the shortest welly boot comes and wrap tape around the stick to mark the point. Now the children need to find a path across the river that all can cross without getting their feet wet, using the stick to help them. The marker tape shows them the maximum height of the water they can walk through.

Lifeline maps: Walk along the watercourse a little way and get the child/ren to imagine it symbolizes their life so far. Then ask them to represent this on the ground with some string. They will need to make it smaller, like a map, but it can still be a few metres long and the same shape as the watercourse. Using what you have brought with you or can find on the ground, ask them what important points they would like to mark and wonder why. Remind them that water keeps on moving, even when it is hard going, just as we do as we get older. When the session ends, you can photograph each of their maps so they have it if they want it and then return the materials you have used to where you found them.

Dams and leaks: One of the favourite activities for children playing in a stream or small river is to create a dam. It gives a very visual metaphor for how feelings can dam up inside us and then sometimes burst through and spill all around. Try different ways to 'channel' the water so it doesn't do this. Allowing a small amount to pass out around the side of the dam tells its own story!

Relaxation: Find a spot to sit or lie, on or near the bank so in a place where you can hear the water. Close your eyes or focus on the sky above. Place your hands on your knees if you are sitting or on your belly if you are lying down and breathe in and out slowly. You can count to four each time you take a breath in and another four when you breathe out.

When your breathing is nice and steady and you don't have to count any more, try to concentrate just on the sound of the water. Let your arms and legs really relax, let your body relax too. If you are concentrating on listening to the water, your mind will begin to relax so you aren't thinking of anything in particular. It might be like the moments just before you fall asleep when you know you are going to but haven't quite got there. You might even fall asleep now, but I will wake you up if you do before we leave to go back and make sure you are safe here too.

One final point to note is that, for children, being anywhere near water generally means getting wet, either by accident or design! A supply of spare clothing including plentiful pairs of socks, an old towel or two, a flask and a snack gives an opportunity to experience care and nurture in a way that children often find easier to accept.

Wood – forests, woodlands, copses and clumps

The term 'wood' is used here to cover a variety of spaces from large areas of forest or woodland – deciduous, coniferous and mixed – to small copses and clumps of trees in school grounds and parks. What follows applies to

Fig 6:8 Woodlands

working in a forest too. The space you use does not have to be huge; a cluster of trees that provides cover and gives the feel of being amongst trunks and branches and immediately surrounded by them works equally as well. *'From their human perspective, it is their constant presence within the community, surviving through one generation to the next and carrying events and stories, that elevate trees to a higher place in our psyche'* (Hight 2011:8).

Woods and forests are fascinating places since they can represent for us both vibrant green life and the dark heart of fairy tales. Imagine lying on your back under the wide spreading canopy of a beech tree, its leaves translucent in the sunshine overhead, glimpses of blue sky in the gaps between the branches and leaves. What finer way to spend an hour or even a few minutes? But how often do we take the time to do this? In our busy lives we can leave taking time to ourselves to the bottom of the 'to do' list. We can forget that there is a plethora of things we can do to restore ourselves which don't cost us much, if any, money but do require us to move out of the house, out of the place of work to seek out a green leafy spot. It may be deep within the countryside or it may be just beyond the door in a park; it may be a small urban courtyard or balcony or simply at the side of the road.

Culturally, trees are seen as symbolic of spiritual growth, union and fertility, physical and spiritual nourishment, liberation and transformation. Psychoanalysis suggests the tree is a symbolic reference to the Mother, to spiritual and intellectual development and to death and rebirth. Seeing trees as maternal symbols, the feminine, arises out of their protective nature, their provision of shade and their giving of nourishment in the form of fruit.

There are many paths and trackways leading into the woods although when you have reached its very heart, they lead away again, back to your own place. They are like the bloodlines in the body, the veins and arteries moving to and from your heart. Pick a pathway and follow it through the trees; through dappled sunlight and sighing branches. On either side, the trees stretch upwards, standing tall like sentinels to mark your way. Their trunks are sometimes rough, cracked and peeling or sometimes soft, clad with moss to show the way when the stars are dimmed and the sun gone.

Underfoot their roots are evident in the pathway, pushing upward through the earth in which they anchor the very heart of the tree, feeding and nourishing it as it pushes towards the light. The roots that catch you unaware beneath your feet are worn smooth by footfalls of humans and the scurrying paws of animals whose homes are deep within the undergrowth and the branches above you. Here too live birds who sweep and swoop between the arms of the trees, tracing their own paths from nest to feeding ground and back again.

Where the darker fir trees live, there is a soft scent in the air and a carpet of fallen needles beneath your tread. The world is darker there, light finds it hard to creep through the closely packed branches and shadows quicken your heartbeat, bringing memories of tales told in childhood.

Overhead where the beeches and oaks stand strong, a green leafy canopy spreads east, west, south and north, shading you from the sun or shielding you from the rain and wind, the wind that may blow like a gentle breeze, ruffling the leaves so they flutter gently, or tear through the very heartland of the wood, tossing the leaves wildly, tearing them from the branches and scattering them across the woodland floor.

I wonder if you ever feel like this, so full of strong energy that you could knock the things around you onto the floor, toss them high and kick them around. Or perhaps sometimes you want to roll up into a ball, to hide away like a hedgehog, tight inside yourself so no-one can reach you. Here in this wood, there are places to hide away where small animals spend their time, sometimes staying still and quiet during the day and coming along the paths at night, feeling bold and brave, seeing in the dark. Sometimes the animals are out and about during the day, just like you; they scamper and play, for-age for a snack and are happy in the sunlight. Then at night, they find their safe place, curl up small and sleep, dreaming of their friends, of running along the trackways or scurrying up a tree. I wonder what you dream of when the sun has done her day's work and the moon has risen to light the night? When we have found our space in woods, you can gather what you find and show me.

When we walk along one of the pathways, tread with your eyes open my friend for sometimes we do not see the root from one of the big old trees whose feet spread so far and wide that they even push up above the sur-face. Take care not to trip, for, as I said, roots can be sneaky and catch you unawares, just as life can! We will travel to the heart of the wood, together, along one of the bloodline pathways. We can listen, look, touch carefully, smell as we go and feel what there is to see!

Getting to know the place

A walk to the woods or into them to the space you are visiting provides an opportunity for using a picture 'map' book and species identification books as described above. Once there, a small copse or areas of trees within school grounds, a park or large garden area may define themselves so that their outer limits become the 'edge' of your play area and form the outer markers of the space the child/ren can use. However, if you are working in a larger area of forest or woodland you will need to mark your working area in some other way, at least until you are sure the children have internalized the map of the space, a process known as 'hefting' in sheep!

Hefting also known as *heafing* is a traditional way to manage sheep grazing on open moorland or common land where communal grazing occurs. Originally, flocks on unfenced land were managed by constant shepherding. Over time, the knowledge or map of the grazing area was passed from ewe to lamb, instilling a lifelong, trans-generational understanding of the best grazing ground and shelter across the year. Anecdotal evidence suggests that because the sheep have a knowledge of and preference for different plants at differing times of the year, this can increase biodiversity. Hefting is traditionally used in areas such as the Lake District, Snowdonia, the Brecon Beacons and Dartmoor.

Using coloured tape or ribbon secured around trees and bushes at the child/ren's chest height provides a very visible marker and is easily put up or removed at the beginnings and ends of sessions if you are working in a public space. Once you are in the space, the child/ren can use the species identification books to look more closely at what is 'natural' to the place, but remind them not to pick anything (see health and safety pointers).

Finding a sit spot is a great starting point for the child/ren using the woods, especially if you are using the same space for each session. It helps to 'ground' them, both in the place where we are and in the session itself. Fearn, writing about therapeutic play in the outdoors, notes:

> A grounded child is absorbed in the present moment, held by gravity between earth and sky, moving freely in response to sensory information from her environment. A child who fully senses who she is in relationship to a special person, and where she is in relationship to a special place, has the inner resources that will support her adolescent curiosity to discover who she is in relationship to other places and other people.
>
> (Fearn 2014:127)

Sitting, squatting or lying with your eyes closed, or with head down or eyes covered by your hand if preferred, focus first on everything you can hear and gradually try to screen out all sounds except one such as birdsong, or the sound of the wind. Breathing slowly and deeply in a regular pattern will help this. If you are working with one child, you can encourage them to match their breathing to yours to help this. If you are working with a group, it's helpful to practise this together beforehand, perhaps using an ocean drum to set the rhythm. Each time you use the sit spot, you can concentrate on a different sense so that you might try to focus on the smell of damp moss, the taste of the wind or raindrops on your tongue, the feel of a leaf or soft moss or closely observe an insect at work.

Health and safety pointers

- When you are working in the woods, tell the children that whatever they are doing, they must be able to see you at all times to avoid getting lost. The area you will have marked out will take account of this.
- When you are risk assessing the space before you take the child/ren there, check for any trip hazards such as tree roots or holes in the ground or low branches or thorny bushes at eye height. Mark them with a visible but safe marker such as a piece of coloured ribbon or tape, a small flexible flag or plastic cone.
- *Know your poisons!* An important part of your risk assessment in any space will be to identify plants, flowers, fruit or fungi which are poisonous or can cause irritation. If you are using your own 'home-made' identification chart, you can create a special section, edged in red, to show those things that must not be touched. However, it is still a good idea to show the child/ren each thing so there is no confusion and, if necessary, mark items with a red ribbon or a small red flag. Also steer clear of any dead animals or droppings even though they may be of interest to the child/ren!
- High winds and even heavy rain can cause damage to twigs and branches which can then pose a hazard to eyes and bodies as they fall to the ground. Your weather check prior to the session will inform you if this is likely. If in doubt – stay out! However, if damage is unlikely, being amongst trees in strong wind can be both exhilarating and scary and is an experience which can take us to the edge of our comfort zone. It also has the ability to create wild energy in children as any teacher will tell you! My mother, a primary school teacher of many years, used to remark that children '*got the wind in their tails*' in such circumstances, making them giddy and lively and even just a little uncontrollable.

Building a nest

If you are working with one child alone, you might use the sit spot as the site for the 'nest', using a small tarpaulin or plastic sheet with a blanket or some soft material to cushion it. Alternatively, you might find a small hollow or space beneath some low hanging branches. You might use a tarpaulin strung between branches or draped over a single one to create a shelter or the cover for a nest. If the child/ren want to build a den, make sure that any supporting structure, or material covering it, is entirely stable and secure before they enter it to avoid it falling in on them.

If you are working with a group and will be using the same space each week, building a story circle is an alternative to a nest. You can construct one either from a number of single logs stood on their round end or longer ones laid along the ground. They will need to be high enough off the ground for the child/ren to sit comfortably on them and stay dry.

Activities

Talking sticks: In Native American culture, trees represent permanence, longevity and a firm base through their roots, provide material for homes and have healing properties. Wood was also used to make talking and prayer sticks.

Talking sticks were used by many of the Native American peoples when a council meeting was called, when holding of the talking stick would allow the council member the opportunity to present their Sacred Point of View, so that only one person speaks at any one time. Talking sticks may also have been used in a powwow session, during storytelling circles, in making decisions in cases of dispute and in any 'meeting' where more than one person would be speaking. Use of the talking stick encourages active listening and ensures that all voices who wish to speak can be heard.

To make a talking stick you will need: A short length of stick 20–30 cm long and at least as thick as your thumb, coloured twine, string or ribbon, beads and feathers. Bind the twine, string or ribbon carefully around the stick, using as many colours as you like, binding over the end of one colour as you start a new colour. Tie the ends securely. If you leave long ends after you have tied them off rather than cutting away the excess, you can add beads and feathers. Make sure the last bead on the thread is securely tied. If you are working with a group, you can use a different child's stick each session when you are talking together or telling stories.

Trust' trails: Using strong twine or rope, the child/ren lay a trail in and around the trees, up and down over mounds and in hollows and over any suitable low branches. The trail should be fairly short to start with but get longer the more confident the child/ren become. Once their trail is laid, they return back along it, using the string to guide them home again. They can either travel with their eyes closed or, if very brave, blindfolded and carefully negotiating the terrain. They may challenge the therapist to do it so be prepared!

Another version of this is to work in pairs with one person blindfolded and the other leading them along the path, where it is safe to do so, back to base. A great activity for building trust in our own abilities, and in the relationships we have made.

Hide and seek: This activity probably needs no introduction! It's really just a different version of 'peek-a-boo' as played with infants, and an activity many of your clients will already play in the playroom. Playing it outdoors adds an extra element for the child/ren because the space is bigger and, to them, the risk of not getting found is greater. Choose a tree to be the base so that it has to be touched before you can be 'home' which allows for the seeker to chase and catch people. Do be clear about how far they can go – I usually say they must be able to see me from where they are hiding.

If you are working with a group and have more than one adult with you, get the children to hide *with* an adult (two or more children per adult if ratio is not 1:1). Getting 'home' is dependent on both the child/ren and the adult sticking together and arriving at the home tree at the same time. Hiding gives an opportunity for experiencing our 'still' body self and how it differs from our 'moving' self.

Tracking and trail laying: Using the natural resources such as sticks, stones and unusual leaves, show the child/ren some examples of how to make signs for trail laying. These need to indicate direction, distance – the number of steps that need to be taken – and any left, right or 'U' turns to be made. Lay a short trail for them to try out, then get them to lay a trail for you to try to follow. Make sure they remember they need to see you from wherever they are.

Mud, glorious mud!: Any areas of mud are likely to be found by the children – they can almost sniff them out! There is nothing so glorious as jumping, stamping, sliding and even rolling in mud. Just make sure you are all wearing old clothes, and if possible waterproofs on top, and have a change of both clothes and footwear if using transport. Also have some water, liquid soap and an old towel for face and hand washing, or baby wipes and anti-bac hand gel for cleaning up after.

Many years ago as a teacher, I took a group of year 1 pupils on an overnight stay at a forest centre nearby. During the day we went for a walk through the forest, along a vehicle track where there were deep pits and ruts. The children kept stopping to delight in jumping in the puddles and squelching in the mud.

That evening, I noticed one of the children was not inside getting ready for supper. I found her, squatted down by a large muddy puddle outside the hut, up to her arms in the squelchy mess, squidging the mud through her fingers. She was the most intellectually developed child in her year group with a reading age way beyond her years and already competently tackling the maths curriculum of key stage 2. Her siblings were similarly 'bright' and her parents extremely pleased with their achievement, with what they could do and how they could think.

The following morning after breakfast, when the other children were getting ready to go out, I again found her in the puddle. She said she didn't want to go with the others, she wanted to stay where she was. Since we had enough staff to allow for this, that was what she did. She played in the muddy water for over an hour, stirring it with a stick, flicking in the air, and generally immersing herself in it. She didn't want any adult participation, she was just content to 'be', a part of her early development that had been by-passed or sacrificed in order that she develop her intellectual capacity.

Climbing trees and swinging on branches are all activities which children seem to want to do. There is something special about being suspended between earth and air, connected only by your arms and unsure of whether you have control over what is going to happen or not! It is exhilarating and at the same time scary, the point we need to experience to know we are truly alive. Being on hand to test the strength of the branches and ready to help is all that is really needed.

Being grounded, connected directly to the earth, feeds our sensory system in a most basic way to enhance our relationship with both ourselves and the space and place around us. As with being in mud, if the child/ren are appropriately dressed, lying, crawling, rolling and slithering like a snake all create the feeling of 'being', our earliest and most basic state, and can allow for access to our deeper, perhaps more troublesome, embodied life metaphors so that they may be brought into conscious awareness and processed through the play.

Earth and air – play parks, school grounds and gardens

Most of us live near a play park and some of us will have a garden attached to the building we are working in. If we are working in schools, the majority of our schools have an outside space even if they don't have a school field.

Fig 6:9 Local play park

Like play parks, some gardens and school grounds may well have some play equipment that can be used. If not, you may be able to rig up a tree swing by using rope of an appropriate thickness which is firmly and safely secured to a strong branch and tested with adult weight. The rope can be knotted at the end in two places with enough space between to allow children to sit on the upper knot with their feet on the lower one to give them support while they hold on with their hands. You might otherwise securely attach an old tyre to the end of the rope for the child/ren to sit on.

The idea for playgrounds originated in Germany where they were attached to schools in order that the children might learn to play properly. There is little information on what constituted 'proper' play but it does rather suggest that the way children played prior to this may have been considered improper! The first public play park built here was in Manchester in 1859. However, Wicksteed Park in Kettering, Northampton, the site of the first slide, built by Charles Wicksteed, also claimed to be the first park of its kind. The slide was a far cry from those of today being basically a wooden ladder, up to 13 feet high with planks descending from it at 45 degree angles. There were no safety railings or rubberized surface below it, just side planks for the top 4 or 5 feet and the hard ground to land on if you fell off! Interestingly, there were separate slides for boys and girls with the tallest slide being for boys only although they are reputed to have used the girls' slides as well. Wicksteed continue to produce playground equipment with their current range including agility playgrounds, outdoor musical instruments and electronic interactive play equipment.

Today, there is a sense that the very carefully designed play park equipment and soft safety surfaces make playing in these places uninteresting and so safe as to be almost risk-free. The Play England document 'Design for Play: A Guide to Creating Successful Play Spaces' (Shackell et al. 2008) outlines ten guiding principles for constructing play spaces, including accessibility for disabled and non-disabled, providing for a range of play experiences and for different ages to play together, making use of natural elements and allowing for change and evolution. The challenge for planners and commissioners of such spaces is to balance out the need for safety against the need for play to contain elements of risk as discussed in chapter 2. When we are taking play therapy sessions into such an environment, we need to have a high degree of trust in our own judgement of what is safe and unsafe, and in our clients' own competence so that we too can balance safety against the need for risk and challenge in play.

Play equipment: swings, slides, roundabouts, rope ladders and scramble nets demand that we use many parts of our bodies to negotiate them holding with our hands, gripping with our legs, pushing them and pulling them, sliding our fronts, backs and bottoms along them, using our feet to stop and start them and using all of us to climb on, up, over and through them. They also offer the opportunity for the child/ren to experience what it is like to be suspended between the earth and the air – to hang in the void. The feeling of the air rushing past our faces as we swing to and fro or whoosh to the bottom of the slide can be both exhilarating and frightening. The giddiness we experience after whirling round and round at a fast pace on the roundabout can be symbolic of the disorientation we feel sometimes when life is unpredictable, or when an event occurs which tests our resilience so we are left like a 'weeble', wobbling badly but not falling down. The moment when we are hanging between earth and air is a moment when we hover on the edge of our tolerance, scared we might fall but wanting to test our nerve and experience the feeling of having done so; a moment when we have to trust our anxious self to our competent self and both to the therapist standing by and when our inner and outer worlds are bridged by the thing we are on and by our own physicality and sense of self.

The therapist was working with a thirteen-year-old boy. During the therapy in the playroom he had been constructing a different and stronger sense of who he was. Deciding to move outside suggested he was ready to face the outside world and test his new self in a more real context. They had since been working outside the playroom in the school play area for five sessions. This space was adjacent to the playroom at one end of a large field used for football and athletics. The play space was set amongst trees which provided a sense of containment of both the area and the play. Within it was a large wooden pirate ship whose hull stood about 8 feet off the ground. Near to it was a large mound with a concrete drainage pipe set in it which the children could pass through. Beyond that was a tall slide which sat on the boundary between the play area and the field although there was no visible marker. The contained play area led to the open field which was edged by a hedge and small trees but was a large 'open' space which the child had so far not used during the sessions. Just beyond the boundary between the two areas was a set of tyres on the ground in the grass which the children had to tip toe through, testing their agility and footwork.

One day, after playing hide and seek on the pirate ship, the boy stood looking out across the grass towards the field. It was a sunny early summer day and it looked inviting. He jumped down from the ship, went up over the mound, scrambled into the drainage pipe and out the other side, went up the steps of the slide, stood for a few seconds before going down and stopping at the bottom to look over the field. He turned to the therapist and said 'Your go now.' She followed his route descending the slide just as he moved back to the bottom of the mound. 'We'll do it together now,' he said, 'me first but you behind me.' They set off again along his chosen route and when the therapist reached the bottom of the slide, the boy turned to her saying 'Come on, this way' and headed towards the tyres. He waited until she was beside him, nimbly negotiated the tyres and then ran out into the field saying 'Come on, this way now, loads of space to play here!' The therapist felt that making a route through the play area which they travelled together to enter the field side by side, the boy had created a 'bridge' between both his inner and outer worlds and one which allowed him to cross from a contained outer world into a bigger, less familiar and somewhat uncontained one, knowing the therapist was at his side. Moving from the playroom, to the contained 'outside' space and then into a wider world was symbolic of the inner journey he had taken, the transformation to his new and stronger sense of competent self and his desire to test it out safely, but in an ever expanding world.

Here we are in the park. People have come here for many years. Children have come with their Mums and Dads, with their Grans and Grandads, with their childminders and their brothers and sisters. They have come here after school, at the weekends, on their contact days and in their holidays. Friends have met each other here and some children have come here alone, sometimes meeting others and joining their play, sometimes staying on the edge of what's happening. I wonder if you have ever stood and watched, unsure of what to do to become part of what's going on? Have you ever had butterflies in your stomach sometimes when you are unsure of what to do?

Children have run across the grass, swung on the swings, twirled on the roundabout and scurried up the cargo netting like spiders. They have plucked up courage to have a go on things that made their stomach turn somersaults and their heads go dizzy and they have hurtled down the slide, shrieking the fear away; shouting and calling to one another. Has that ever happened to you? Have you wanted to shout out loud and scream so the whole world can hear you?! Or do you prefer to hide away and watch the world from a secret place?

How are you feeling today? Will you stand and watch and wait until you see what others are doing or are you feeling ready to have a go at something new? Maybe you just want to run across the grass, feeling the freedom it offers when there is nothing in your way. You might feel the wind in your face, the up and down of the ground below and the moment when you are not quite up in the air or down on the ground but in that place in between. You can get that feeling on the other things here, especially on the swings. One minute you're flying up into the air and the next your feet are almost touching the ground. We will be here together, so when you are ready you can show me what you would like to do.

Getting to know the place

The child/ren may already be familiar with the space you are using so it is interesting for them to have their attention drawn to unfamiliar aspects or things they may not naturally notice about familiar things. You can use a 'Can you spot?' list to do this, or turn it into a game, similar to 'I Spy', so that you ask each other in turn, 'Can you spot, hear or smell something?'

Children often have one or two favourite pieces of equipment they like to go on so a game of 'follow my leader' in which you have to travel on, up, down, through or over each thing can also help to familiarize them with everything that is within the space. You can also do this activity using a map book to guide the child/ren around a trail you have set and combine two activities by giving them a 'Can you spot?' list at the same time.

Health and safety pointers

- Part of our risk assessment process is checking that any equipment we are using is sound and safe. It is always useful to do this, even in a public park, and not to assume that because it's a public space, all will be well. Unless someone reports broken or hazardous things, they won't get fixed. School equipment is usually checked by the site manager but still worth checking yourself before a session. Guidance about litter given earlier will apply here.
- Additional limitations you set in this environment may depend on the age and physical competence of the child/ren. When your job is to keep everyone safe, the top of the cargo net or the roof of the fort may seem a long way above the ground. You may find your own heart pounding! Be clear in your own mind about your tolerance levels and set clear limits at the start of the session to support these. This is more helpful than trying to put something in place when your own anxiety levels are raised and the child/ren sense your mounting panic. If the park has a large open area in addition to the play area, pick obvious boundary markers or use a rope to indicate the area you are working in.
- Take care when you and the child/ren are moving from one place to another if there are others using the play park. Give swings a wide berth, don't start off down the slide when someone else is still on it and don't try to get on or off the roundabout while it's still going. (And there's a lesson in life for all of us in that statement!) The guidelines about dogs given in the 'Water' section of this chapter may also apply here if you are not in a dog-free area.

Building a nest

Play parks often have benches and picnic tables which can be used as the 'nesting' point if it is difficult to construct something on the ground or in a more secluded area. A bird's nest swing is ideal, especially if you have the

Fig 6:10 Bird's nest swing – an ideal therapy nest!

space to yourselves (see fig 6:10). Otherwise, the child/ren may choose to use a piece of equipment such as a wooden castle, fort or ship, or an area beneath a fixed structure. How possible this is will depend on whether or not there are other children around and how easy it is to keep the space for yourselves. Since the nest is the gathering point, both in terms of meeting and of 'gathering' thoughts, the quieter the area you can find, the better. A seat in a quiet part of the park or away from the play area will do. I have used the walk back to base as the time when we reflect on the session as, for many children, being side by side and moving makes verbal communication more comfortable and feels less intrusive. If you are using a public space, you may want to structure your routine to include time back in the quietness of the playroom to end your time together.

The journey to and from the space you will be visiting is equally a part of the session. Whether you travel on foot or in a minibus, it is time when you are often close, next to each other, and in transition between here and there, now and then. It is a space between the outer world or the playground space and the inner world of the playroom. Movement also seems to free up some children to talk, as if when the body is occupied, connecting up the actions to promote movement, our mind and our thought processes are also free to be active and make connections.

Activities

Stride like a giant: As was noted in chapter 5, the world is not generally proportioned to the size of children and they can often feel quite small in relation to the environments they are in. Moving with powerful, strong movements gives them a sense of the strength they have and how to use it positively. Ask the child/ren to try to walk like a big, powerful, striding giant. What noise do they think the giant would make? How big would its strides be and how would it move its arms? Would it move quietly or would the footsteps be heavy, and shake the ground all around? Then ask them to move like a little, frightened animal that has just seen the giant. How fast would it go and in which direction? How would it move and what sound, if any, might it make? How might it feel to be the little creature? Ask them to switch between the two. You can encourage reflection on which character the child/ren would rather be and why and how it felt to move from one to the other.

Rope walking: Get the children to help you to lay a long thick rope along the ground with wiggles and bends in it. See if the child/ren can walk along it taking small 'heel to toe' steps. Then let them find other ways of travelling along it, altering the stride length and speed of movement. If you are working with a group, the children can start individually but then join together to complete the course. If the weather and ground conditions are suitable, they can do this activity in their socks or bare feet and experience the feeling of gripping with bare toes.

Carry the water: This activity was developed with a group of boys when working in a play park next to a shallow stream. Working in pairs, the object of the activity is to transport a bucket of water along an obstacle course without spilling any. While you fill the buckets (from a tap or with water you have carried with you) the child/ren work out a course around the play equipment as simple or as complex as they like. You will need to pass the bucket back and forth between you in order to negotiate the obstacles. Be prepared to get wet!

Miniature gardens: You will need some shallow trays, a small trowel or an old spoon and some sand, soil or compost. The children fill the trays with a layer of soil and, using what they can find around them, create a miniature garden that they would like to spend time in. This is a timeless activity which I first did when I was in the Brownies, but children love creating small worlds of entirely their own making as we see when they use the sand tray.

Other timeless activities that my clients have enjoyed immensely are games like football, cricket, rounders and Frisbee. They allow them to demonstrate their skill, to beat us and manipulate the rules, all ways of experimenting with personal power, and often these games bring out their playful shadow side as they hurl the Frisbee or the ball at you, knowing it is going to make you run or dive!

Fire

In Greek mythology, the phoenix, a magnificent bird with shimmering feathers the colour of sunrise lived for the longest of times. When its time of death approached, the story tells us that it would build a nest of aromatic wood, and burn in the flames of the fire. A new phoenix would arise from the ashes. Fire is both the creator and the destroyer and symbolizes passion, energy and renewal. It is the only element that can be made by humans and so is thought to bridge the worlds of the mortals and gods. Across time and cultures, people have built campfires to give warmth and light, to boil water and cook food. The campfire would keep wild animals at bay and is said to have warded off evil spirits. It is the focus of the meeting circle used by many peoples down through time. If you are able to have a campfire in the space you are using, particularly if you are working with a group, the child/ren will get very excited, be mesmerized by its flames, driven back by its smoke which has a habit of shifting around the circle, and want to add fuel to it constantly. It will become a focal point and once you are confident with it and have the right safety equipment, nothing is better on a cold day than hot chocolate and marshmallows, prepared on the campfire.

Gather round the fire to warm yourselves. Enter through the gate we have made and sit safely on the seats to gaze into the bright flames. Sometimes they leap high, roaring as they go and lighting up the trees around us. At other times they flicker and dance like the flame of a candle in the breeze. If the wind blows, the smoke may shift and follow you, stinging your eyes and chasing you around the circle as you try to escape it.

If you watch the flames, you can see patterns and shapes, see them form and shift and become a different one, all in a split second. Sometimes the flames are bright yellows and oranges, but as you look towards the heart of the fire where it is hottest, they become red and glow more brightly as if this is the very life of it. If it rains, you may hear the fire hiss and sizzle as the raindrops turn to steam and are gone in an instant.

As we come to the end of our time together, we let the fire die down. The heat will begin to fade, and the flames will be gone but the embers will glow, in the heart of it, where the life is. The embers will stay warm for a long while. When we pour water over them to cool them down, it will bubble and boil as it runs across them sending great clouds of stream and smoke about us. And long after we have left and returned home, the smell of the fire will still be with us, reminding us of our time together. Can you smell it on your clothes and in your hair? Perhaps it will still be on you tomorrow when you wake up. I wonder what other smells there are which remind you of a time or a place you have passed through or a person you have known?

Health and safety pointers

- If you are going to use fire, you need to be confident with it yourself, in starting it, maintaining it and extinguishing it.
- If you are working on a beach you will need to check first that fires are allowed.
- If you are working in a public space where other people are around, a fire is not appropriate.
- If you are working on 'private' land such as in school grounds, then again you need to check that you can have a fire.
- If you are going to prepare food or drinks, you need the proper safety equipment.

Basic equipment is listed on the resources list in appendix 4. What follows is guidance only. You are advised to seek training in using fire and fire pits and for the appropriate first aid procedures for burns.

On the beach

- Create a fire pit by placing a grill over a hole in the sand. The fire will be set on the grill and the embers and bits of smouldering fuel will fall into it.
- Draw a circle in the sand at least 2 metres from the pit at all points.
- Get the children to build a wall of sand on the perimeter line, mounding up additional sand on top of this to make seats.
- Create a door in the wall. Children can only enter the circle through this door and only at the invitation of the therapist who sits opposite the door to face those coming in. This can form part of your welcome ritual. As they enter, they move along the perimeter wall to a seat. No one crosses the fire circle.
- If you are going to allow the children to add fuel to the fire or toast marshmallows you must have fireproof gloves available for them to use.
- For doing either of these activities, teach the *'respect'* position – kneeling on one knee – to avoid them losing their balance and toppling into the fire.
- Tell the children nothing gets **thrown** on the fire.
- Have at least 20 litres of salt water ready to hand to extinguish the fire. Make sure the children have left the fire circle before you put the fire out as it will steam and smoke.
- On the beach, the embers should then be buried so they are not a hazard to other beach users or, if the tide is incoming, they can be scattered at its edge.
- *Have a burns kit to hand and know how to apply it.*

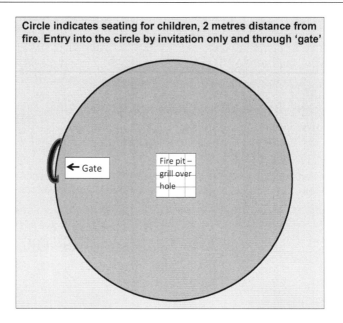

Fig 6:11 How to construct a fire pit

On land (not for use in a public space)

Once your fire is extinguished, you will need to be clear about how you ensure no-one else goes near the circle until the embers are cold. Do this <u>BEFORE</u> you light the fire so you do not leave it unattended without knowing it will be safe.

- Remove turf from a square of grass to safeguard it and create a pit at least 20 cm deep. Surround the pit with stones or thick logs to mark the edge clearly.
- Follow the guidance above but use logs to create the perimeter and form the seating.
- Don't forget to leave a 'door' in the log circle and use the same procedure for entry.
- Have the same amount of water on hand for putting it out, using rainwater where possible. Do this only when the children have left the circle. Pour some of the water on, then rake the embers over with a long log and pour more water on. Repeat this until all the embers are soaked. **Make sure you have made everyone who needs to know aware that you have used the fire circle and that the embers are still warm.**

Small spaces and other places

You don't need to access a large space to be working in nature. She inhabits the smallest of spaces, right down to a crack in the pavement where a single dandelion grows. Any safe outside space can be used although you may have to adapt activities if space is restricted. Small spaces which have been used include:

- a walled and concreted area just beyond the children's ward of a hospital
- a grassed area behind a CAMHS building
- an area of garden next to a children's centre
- a paved area outside a café
- an area of tarmac beyond the special needs hut in a school

Where possible, the areas have been softened by the addition of some pots of plants, unsightly walls have been festooned with fabric and hard surfaces covered with rubber matting and picnic blankets. You can gather natural resources such as shells, pebbles and interesting fallen wood and branches from other places and transport them in. Logs can be used as seating and low-level coffee tables provide a raised area for collage work. In all these spaces,

Fig 6:12 A small garden space

you can generally still feel the rain, wind and sun on your skin and the sounds, smells and textures nature provides will be there, if you look for them.

Towns and villages often have community resources, a considerable number the result of millennium funding. You may be able to use a village hall, and many of these have green space around them as part of their plot. More and more community gardens and orchards are springing up as a result of the growing desire to reconnect with nature and virtually every community has a children's play park of some description. Remember the saying, 'seek and ye shall find'.

I want to leave you leave you with a story from a colleague of mine that underlines how moving to work in nature can really facilitate a deeper level of working. This is the story of an eleven-year-old girl who had been working with her therapist, a therapeutic social worker for just under a year. Life for her was chaotic and the relationship with her therapist offered one of the few points of stability for her. The therapist takes up the story.

I started off doing fairly structured direct work with this client but quite quickly I realized the way to build a relationship with her was to work in a much more non-directive way. We did quite a few weeks of non-directive play and it was during the period when we were moving around from venue to venue when we became homeless from our office. She was in her third foster placement but it ended and she was moved to a different one which was on the other side of the city. Initially the foster carers were bringing her over to our offices but they had little understanding of her needs and were not happy about bringing her on a half an hour journey across to see me. They made it clear that it was an inconvenience as they also had another child in the placement.

And also I guess there was pressure on the room where we were because of the impending move so we tended to work in the lounge at the centre which didn't have a full range of resources. It was quite difficult in that room really to just do non-directive stuff so we ended up doing more structured things like cooking which I felt was all a bit kind of artificial. She had a nice time and I used to try and do some really nurturing things with her. I would give her hand massages and paint her nails but it was becoming increasingly difficult with the carers' reluctance to bring her over to the centre so I started picking her up and because the traffic was appalling, by the time we got back it was practically time to take her home again. So I decided we would actually try to work outdoors and I knew from her previous placement the things she really liked doing were going for walks and splashing around in the mud in her wellies and climbing trees. She had a pair of wellies but she wasn't allowed to get them muddy and it was a very sterile environment in the house with leather sofas and a big telly and no evidence of games or toys. It all felt very controlled. I thought that maybe we should go outside because we've just got this hour before I've got to get her back to school and there's lots of big green open spaces over this side of the city and there's the sea although it's not particularly lovely, not like your sea or the sea we went to on your day! So we started going to one of the local country parks which has lots of woodland and green areas and a bit of a grotty kind of beach and she just absolutely loved it! We'd go and we'd just try to go for a walk really and explore and she just really loved it. She just relaxed! Being outside and just being in a different environment concentrating on different things – it was winter so quite often it would rain – concentrating on the wind and the rain in our faces and how loud the waves were and how muddy the path was just kind of freed her up to really start expressing how things were at home and how she felt about things. So things kind of shifted really, I suppose.

The elemental aspect of it, listening to the waves, focusing on the wind on your face, all kind of allowed her to connect more with the idea of changes and shifts, in emotions. Yes, I think she worried a bit about the weather, she didn't have the gear. I had to lend her wellies and stuff and often in the course of the hour or hour and a half that we'd be out it would be raining when I picked her up but by the time we got to where we were going the sun would be out and of course the weather could change several times while we were out and of course that kind of mirrored her ... she was just pretty all over the place and I think something about that sharing the experience of the elements and the physicality of it all helped with the shift in her.

(Foskett 2016)

References

Bennett, S. (26th November 2012) Sky Patterson finds a metaphor for life in water. *San Antonio Express News.* Available from: www.mysanantonio.com/lifestyle/art-icle/Sky-Patterson-finds-a-metaphor-for-life-in-water-4062240.php [Accessed 3rd January 2017]

Fearn, M. (2014) Working therapeutically with groups in the outdoors: A natural space for healing. In Prendiville, E. and Howard, J. (eds) *Play Therapy Today: Contemporary Practice with Individuals, Groups and Carers.* Abingdon: Routledge

Fekete, A and Haidari, R. (2015) Special aspects of water use in Persian gardens. *Acta Universitatis Sapientiae Agriculture and Environment* 7 (2015), 82–88. Available from: doi: 10.1515/ausae-2015-0007 [Accessed 14th October 2016]

Foskett, L. (2016) Interview with Alison Chown, 10 September

Gietz, W. (2014) *The 5 Qualities of the Perfect 'Sit Spot'.* Available from: http://weare-wildness.com/5-qualities-perfect-sit-spot/ [Accessed 20th December 2016]

Hight, J. (2011) *Britain's Tree Story: The History and Ancient Legends of Britain's Trees.* England: National Trust Books

Shackell, A., Butler, N., Doyle, P. and Ball, D. (2008) *Design for Play: A Guide to Creating Successful Play Spaces.* Available from: www.playengland.org.uk/media/70684/design-for-play.pdf [Accessed 23rd September 2016]

Appendix 1

The issue of competency

For a fuller discussion of competency and confidentiality see Chown (2014:139–145).

Jordan (2015:84) in discussing working outdoors with adult clients suggests the rationale for moving outdoors depends on the 'unique' work that is going on with the client and that the decision to move outside and the setting up of the therapeutic contract can be negotiated with the client. Whilst the Children Act of 1989 encourages the participation of children in decision making, we need to recognize those factors which are crucially different to working with adults, principally that unless a child or young person is able to understand all the issues that arise from or will be a consequence of their decision, they are not deemed as fully competent to make an autonomous decision about any treatment they may have access to, including therapy; hence consent from those who have legal responsibility for the child or young person must be given in order for the therapy to take place. Fionda (2009) suggests this idea of being competent, or having sufficient mental capacity, takes into account maturity, powers of reasoning and intelligence.

This is helpful in avoiding the notion that there is an age-related cut-off point after which a child is deemed competent to make an autonomous decision, although there is general agreement that for those children following a more typical developmental pathway, they are beginning to be 'competent' somewhere around the age of ten (the age of criminal responsibility) or eleven. It does mean, however, that play therapists must use their professional judgement about the reality of children's participation, alongside discussion with those others who have responsibility for the child's safety and well-being and I would anticipate that such discussions take place prior to the commencement of the therapy. As previously mentioned, this does not mean that there is no scope for negotiation with the client, rather that we need to have a full understanding of our responsibility towards a child and their ability to make decisions for themselves. The Ethical Basis for Good Practice in Play Therapy (BAPT 2014) in highlighting the need to respect people's rights and dignity tells us that:

Play Therapists seek freely the informed consent of those legally responsible for clients and, where possible, assent from clients, … [and] … are aware that special safeguards may be necessary to protect the rights and welfare of clients who are non-autonomous and dependent on significant others.

Children's ability to consent to treatment is enshrined in the 'Gillick competency and Fraser guidelines'. These emanate from a 1980s court case between Gillick and West Norfolk & Wisbeck Area Health Authority when Mrs Victoria Gillick questioned the right of doctors to give contraceptive advice to a young person under the age of sixteen. The guidelines state that:

whether or not a child is capable of giving the necessary consent will depend on the child's maturity and understanding and the nature of the consent required. The child must be capable of making a reasonable assessment of the advantages and disadvantages of the treatment proposed, so the consent, if given, can be properly and fairly described as true consent.

(Gillick v West Norfolk & Wisbeck Area Health Authority 1986)

References

BAPT (2014) *Ethical Basis for Good Practice in Play Therapy.* Available from: www.bapt.info/play-therapy/ethical-basis-good-practice-play-therapy/ [Accessed 27th August 2016]

Chown, A. (2014) *Play Therapy in the Outdoors: Taking Play Therapy out of the Playroom and into Natural Environments.* London: Jessica Kingsley Publishers

Fionda, J. (2009) Children, young people and the law. In Montgomery, H. and Kellet, M. (eds) *Children and Young People's Worlds: Developing Frameworks for Integrated Practice.* Bristol: Policy Press

Gillick v West Norfolk & Wisbeck Area Health Authority [1986] AC 112 House of Lords. Available from: www.e-lawresources.co.uk/cases/Gillick-v-West-Norfolk.php [Accessed 2nd September 2016]

Jordan, M. (2015) *Nature and Therapy: Understanding Counselling and Psychotherapy in Outdoor Spaces.* Hove: Routledge

Appendix 2

Health and safety – practical considerations

Insurance

For the purposes of insurance, *professional indemnity* insurance protects us if clients have to be compensated for loss or damage as a result of negligent advice or services we have provided as an individual or business, whilst *public liability* covers the cost of compensation claims for personal injury or damage to or loss of the property of members of the public (Association of British Insurers 2014a, 2014b). If you are already insured, you will need to contact your insurers to check whether or not you are covered for outdoor work otherwise you will need an initial discussion to outline your insurance needs and will find it helpful to check with your professional association about any specific requirements for registration.

First aid

Good quality first aid training is a useful thing to have and, under our safe-guarding duties, we need to ensure that when we take children 'off-site', that is away from the normal setting of our work, we do so safely and avoiding as much risk as possible. Whilst most training organizations can offer basic first aid courses, there are those which will provide training specifically aimed at those working in outdoor environments. However, if you are employed by a school or other organization or agency, you will need to discuss the administering of first aid with them as they may have a particular procedure involving their designated first aider. They may also wish to include you in any first aid training given to staff but it is important to consider what you need in order to feel confident to cope with unforeseen incidents particularly since not all risk can be removed from every situation. If the child needs medication of any sort, again this must be discussed fully with the employing organization or with those with parental responsibility, particularly if need for medicines is not predictable, since there are strict guidelines around the administering of such medications.

Safeguarding

Safeguarding is a complex issue and it is beyond the scope of this chapter to discuss it in full detail. However, comprehensive guidance is contained in the document 'Working Together to Safeguard Children – A Guide to Inter-agency Working to Safeguard and Promote the Welfare of Children' (2015) which can be obtained from www.gov.uk. Responsibility for defining arrangements in each local authority rests with Local Safeguarding Children Boards (LSCB). However, the guidance also notes that '*Whilst local authorities play a lead role, safeguarding children and protecting them from harm is everyone's responsibility. Everyone who comes into contact with children and families has a role to play*' (HM Government 2015:5). Safeguarding is the broader 'umbrella' term under which 'child protection' sits and the Royal College of Paediatrics and Child Health (RCPCH) offers a helpful distinction between the two, reminding us that whilst safeguarding is concerned with promoting the welfare of young people, child protection refers to the activities undertaken to prevent identified children suffering from or likely to suffer significant harm as a result of abuse or neglect (RCPCH 2014).

So, safeguarding is defined as the action that is taken to promote the welfare of children and protect them from harm and applies to all those under the age of eighteen. It encompasses the notion of protecting children from abuse and maltreatment, preventing harm to their health and development, ensuring they grow up with the provision of safe and effective care and ensures that action is taken to enable all those up to the age of eighteen to have the best outcomes. Safeguarding legislation and guidance requires all those who work with children and young people to have safeguarding policies and procedures in place, including safe recruiting policies and practices. If they are employers, they need to ensure all staff are effective at consistently applying these and that they receive relevant up-to-date safeguarding training. Employers are also required to have procedures for dealing with concerns and managing any allegations made against staff or volunteers.

In addition to everyone's responsibility to ensure children and young people are safeguarded from harm, professional organizations such as BAPT, PTUK, BACP and UKCP have ethical standards for good practice which include the concepts of *beneficence* and *non-maleficence*. Beneficence requires us to always act with the best interests of the client in mind and to promote their well-being, whilst non-maleficence requires us to make a commitment to avoid doing harm to our clients, both of which serve to underline our safeguarding responsibilities. If you are employed by a school or other organization or agency, you will need to adhere to their safeguarding policies and practices and be familiar with how these apply to your therapeutic sessions both inside and outdoors, particularly since therapists are in a somewhat unique position in today's culture in that whereas most workers are advised to avoid being in a room on their own with a child, paradoxically therapists insist on it. This makes it all the more important that we are fully aware of our safeguarding responsibilities and our professional organization's codes of conduct and good practice.

Duty of care

Duty of care is a legal term with which we may be familiar. Broadly speaking, it underlines our safeguarding responsibilities in that it is defined as the 'legal obligation to safeguard others from harm while they are in your care, using your services or exposed to your activities' (Collins Dictionary 2016). For employers, it means that they must take all steps which are reasonably possible to ensure the health, safety and well-being of their employees and includes both physical and mental health. If you are employed by a school or other organization or agency this would extend to you and if you run your own organization, the legal responsibility to ensure a duty of care to your employees would rest with you.

Whilst duty of care is a legal obligation, as an employer one might wish to ensure the physical and mental well-being of one's employees because it is the right thing to do and because it fosters the best working relationships and models 'best working practice'.

Whatever category of worker we are, commissioned, contracted or self-employed, we also have a duty of care to ourselves in that it is imperative that we look to support our own sense of well-being by not working when we are unwell and by taking time to relax and recuperate so we achieve a reasonable work/life balance. Because we are also working with and containing the strong emotions and distress of our clients, rebalancing our own energies is important whether through personal therapy, supervision or activities which enhance our own playful self or a combination of all three.

Weather

Once you decide you are going to take your play therapy practice into nature, you need to be prepared to go out in all but the severest weathers! Depending on the environment available to you, a general rule of thumb is that stormy conditions with high winds are problematic but wet or cold weather is not although since you will be carrying out your own risk assessment of each environment, this will naturally include the weather conditions on the day. The key to being able to be out is appropriate clothing which the child brings with them or which the setting you are working in provides. You might decide to have spare warm and waterproof clothing for your clients but bear in mind they come in a variety of sizes and, for safety reasons, appropriate outdoor clothing needs to be fairly close fitting rather than oversized or tight. The issue of risk assessment will be discussed in Appendix 3 but it is worth mentioning here that rain equals wet grass which can be very slippery and if the environment you are using is fully grassed, any risk assessment will need to take account of this.

A note about cleaning resources

Health and safety recommendations suggest we need to ensure toys and equipment are cleaned with anti-bacterial substances in order to avoid cross-contamination and that sand should be changed regularly. Clients should be encouraged to avoid hand to mouth contact. They also suggest clients are given sanitizing wipes or gel to clean their hands at the beginning and end of a session. When working in nature, this is perhaps doubly crucial as is your own knowledge of what flora and fauna are poisonous and it is part of our duty of care to ensure we are appropriately informed. Avoid using ground contaminated by animal faeces but be particularly aware of dog faeces as they are especially hazardous and can cause serious infections.

References

Association of British Insurers (2014a) *Professional Indemnity Insurance*. Available from: www.abi.org.uk/Insurance-and-savings/Products/Business-insurance/Liability-insurance/Professional-indemnity-insurance [Accessed 14th September 2016]

Association of British Insurers (2014b) *Public Liability Insurance*. Available from: www.abi.org.uk/Insurance-and-savings/Products/Business-insurance/Liability-insurance/Public-liability-insurance [Accessed 14th September 2016]

Collins Dictionary (2016) Available from: www.collinsdictionary.com/dictionary/english [Accessed 11th September 2016]

HM Government (2015) *Working Together to Safeguard Children: A Guide to Interagency Working to Safeguard and Promote the Welfare of Children*. Available from: www.gov.uk/government/uploads/system/uploads/attachment_data/file/419595/Working_Together_to_Safeguard_Children.pdf [Accessed 12th September 2016]

Royal College of Paediatrics and Child Health (2014) *Safeguarding Children and Young People: Roles and Competences for Health Care Staff*: [Intercollegiate document] Available from: www.rcpch.ac.uk/sites/default/files/page/Safeguarding%20Children%20-%20Roles%20and%20Competences%20for%20Healthcare%20Staff%20%2002%200%20%20%20%20(3)_0.pdf [Accessed 10th September 2016]

Risk assessment

It is beyond the scope of this chapter to give full guidance on the process of risk assessment and it is advisable to get advice from the school, agency or other organizations you are employed by so that you are familiar with both their policy and preferred practice. There is, however, a wealth of guidance available from relevant organizations, some of which may also provide basic training in risk assessment. The Education Scotland website provides us with a clear definition of the basic process:

> Risk assessment is a process that identifies and assesses the importance of risk in a situation and then assesses the measures that control it. It is the process that is important. Any written risk assessment is simply evidence that an appropriate process has been gone through. (Educationscotland no date)

This definition is helpful because it underlines the idea that it is the process of looking at an environment, identifying the potential hazards, calculating the risk of harm and taking steps to reduce that harm which is important and, as responsible play therapists, we will already be applying this process to the playrooms in which we work. We will have looked around the room and identified things that might be tripped over, sharp corners that might cause injury, slippery surfaces which are underfoot and we will have made sure that the toys and other resources we have in the room are child-friendly and not likely to be toxic or cause harm in other ways. This will be part of the almost unconscious process we go through when we set out with a new client or work in an unfamiliar space. It is within our duty of care and part of upholding our responsibility to act with beneficence and non-maleficence.

When we move into outdoor spaces, we continue to apply this process of identifying hazards, those things which may cause harm, and calculating risk, the likelihood of someone being harmed by those hazards, and how serious the harm might be. The Health and Safety Executive (HSE 2002) suggests three levels of risk assessment:

- **General risk assessment** – those inherent in an activity and which are written
- **Site specific risk assessment** – those associated with the particular site which are also written
- **Dynamic risk assessment** – risks occurring at the time of the activity such as changing conditions and fitness of those involved which are physical, mental and attitudinal. This dynamic assessment needs to continue throughout the activity.

So we will not only be looking at the physical state of the environment – the general terrain in which we are planning to work – but also considering things such as the weather, our clients' health and welfare including appropriate clothing, who or what else might come into close proximity including things such as wandering dogs or plants with poisonous berries or sharp thorns, and any transport we might be using or which we might meet.

We might also add to this by considering the idea of risk/benefit assessment where the benefit from the activity is balanced against the managed risk in undertaking it. If we believe there is a clear benefit for the client from play therapy sessions in outdoor spaces, and we carry out the appropriate risk assessment and undertake any subsequent actions to reduce risk, then we are acting with the best interests of the client in mind. Since any assessment is designed to reduce risk to an acceptable level, how well we know the environment we are working in and how at ease we feel in it are an integral part of the process so we need to take time to become familiar with any new place. Becoming familiar with an environment includes being aware of the significance it might hold for us, the meaning it has and the relationship we have with it. Spending time in quiet meditation in the place where the therapy will take place will enable us to attune to these aspects of our own process so that when we are there with our client we can be fully attuned to them.

References

Educationscotland (no date) *Planning Outdoor Learning – Health and Safety Guides.* Available from: www.educationscotland.gov.uk/learningandteaching scotland [Accessed 23rd August 2016]

Health and Safety Executive (2002) *Glenridding Beck – Investigation Report.* Available from: www.hse.gov.uk/aala/glenridding-beck-investigation.pdf [Accessed 2nd September 2016]

Appendix 4

Resources

The items listed below are in addition to any resources you take from the play-room. You may not need to take all of the items with you for each session but you may need all of them at some point.

- mobile phone with appropriate network coverage
- large sheets of plastic or a tarpaulin
- rope
- strong string or twine
- tent pegs
- tent awning poles
- small sheets of plastic for sitting on
- blanket/s or fabric for nesting
- different coloured garden twine for binding
- feathers
- beads
- coloured ribbon, small flags and/or cones for hazard marking
- coloured sticky tape
- gaffer tape
- walking pole
- identification books – commercial and homemade
- homemade map books
- camera
- small sketch pads, pencils and pens
- spades and trowels
- bivvy bag – survival bag available from outdoor equipment retailers
- buckets
- water, soap, small towel, hand sanitizing gel
- baby wipes or anti-bac wipes
- small roll of toilet paper or tissues
- first aid kit (including sun screen)

If you are building a campfire:

- firelighters
- matches or Swedish fire-lighting steel
- fireproof gloves for children and adults
- burns kit
- long, firm sticks for toasting marshmallows
- water for extinguishing fire

Appendix 5

Can you spot ... hear or smell?

- Three different thing.s growing on the bank
- An animal that lives near the river
- Something coming from a farm
- Something touching the water – not the bank!
- Three different birds
- Something that lives in the water
- Something from a factory
- Three different types of tree
- Signs of animal homes along the bank
- Something that tells you lots of people are nearby
- Three things that shouldn't be here
- Something that tells you that you can get food near here
- Something that tells you people come here to fish
- Two different ways of crossing the river
- Three things that can float

Appendix 6

Can you spot ... hear ... smell ... touch?

- Can you spot three different flowers?
- Can you touch something smooth and shiny?
- Can you spot an even smaller play area for little children?
- Can you smell any food cooking?
- Can you hear some vehicles?
- Can you touch something rough?
- Can you spot some vegetables growing?
- Can you smell something unpleasant?!
- Can you hear some other children?
- Can you touch something that feels a bit hairy?

- Walk along the fence all around the field with me:
    - How many houses can you spot?
    - What animals can you hear?
    - What can you smell?

Appendix 7

Checklist for general preparation

In advance of session

☐ Discussion with supervisor.

☐ Space/s visited, sit spot found, observations taken.

☐ Consideration of any limitations needed.

☐ Parental permission agreed including any specific points – e.g., allergies, medication and/or first aid administration, physical contact, additional and/or personal care needs, cultural considerations.

☐ Risk/benefit assessment undertaken, any necessary adaptions for additional needs made, shelter spot identified, toileting needs considered alternative/safety route identified if appropriate.

☐ Therapist kit assembled (see additional checklists) including mobile phone with appropriate network coverage.

☐ Resources from playroom agreed and in transportable, waterproof containers.

On the day of the session

☐ Check mobile phone is fully charged and first aid kit and therapist hygiene kit topped up.

☐ Check site for litter and other harmful debris.

☐ Check weather forecast, is site still appropriate? If so, what additional clothing or resources may be needed? If not, which location will be used, if any? Check alternative site as above.

☐ Pack any refreshments if appropriate.

☐ Gather playroom, and any other, resources needed.

☐ Ensure child has appropriate clothing and footwear for weather and play activities.

Your own checklist items

☐

☐

☐

☐

☐

☐

☐

☐

Appendix 8

Some useful websites

- http://archimedes-earth.com/course-list/forest-schools/
- www.childrenandnature.org/
- www.forestry.gov.uk/
- www.forestschoolassociation.org/what-is-forest-school/
- www.letthechildrenplay.net/
- www.metoffice.gov.uk/public/weather/forecast/
- www.metoffice.gov.uk/public/weather/tide-times/
- www.nationaltrust.org.uk/children-and-nature
- https://naturenurture.org.uk/
- www.nature-play.co.uk/
- www.playengland.org.uk/media/71062/charter-for-childrens-play.pdf
- www.redcross.org.uk/What-we-do/First-aid/First-aid-training
- https://rethinkingchildhood.com/tag/nature-play/

Index

Taylor & Francis eBooks

Helping you to choose the right eBooks for your Library

Add Routledge titles to your library's digital collection today. Taylor and Francis ebooks contains over 50,000 titles in the Humanities, Social Sciences, Behavioural Sciences, Built Environment and Law.

Choose from a range of subject packages or create your own!

Benefits for you

» Free MARC records
» COUNTER-compliant usage statistics
» Flexible purchase and pricing options
» All titles DRM-free.

REQUEST YOUR FREE INSTITUTIONAL TRIAL TODAY

Free Trials Available
We offer free trials to qualifying academic, corporate and government customers.

Benefits for your user

» Off-site, anytime access via Athens or referring URL
» Print or copy pages or chapters
» Full content search
» Bookmark, highlight and annotate text
» Access to thousands of pages of quality research at the click of a button.

eCollections – Choose from over 30 subject eCollections, including:

Archaeology	Language Learning
Architecture	Law
Asian Studies	Literature
Business & Management	Media & Communication
Classical Studies	Middle East Studies
Construction	Music
Creative & Media Arts	Philosophy
Criminology & Criminal Justice	Planning
Economics	Politics
Education	Psychology & Mental Health
Energy	Religion
Engineering	Security
English Language & Linguistics	Social Work
Environment & Sustainability	Sociology
Geography	Sport
Health Studies	Theatre & Performance
History	Tourism, Hospitality & Events

For more information, pricing enquiries or to order a free trial, please contact your local sales team:
www.tandfebooks.com/page/sales

Routledge
Taylor & Francis Group

The home of
Routledge books

www.tandfebooks.com